Images
Into
The
Mind

A Radical New Look At Understanding And Changing Behavior

Daniel G. Amen, M.D.

MindWorks Press
350 Chadbourne Road
Fairfield, California 94585
(707) 429-7181

ISBN 1-886554-01-3
Manufactured in the United States of America
9 8 7 6 5 4

Other Books By Dr. Amen

WINDOWS INTO THE A.D.D. MIND:
Understanding and Treating Attention Deficit Disorder
Childhood Through Adulthood

DON'T SHOOT YOURSELF IN THE FOOT
A Program To End Self-Defeating Behavior Forever

THE INSTRUCTION MANUAL THAT SHOULD HAVE COME WITH YOUR CHILD
New Skills for Frazzled Parents

HEALING THE CHAOS WITHIN
The Interaction Between A.D.D., Alcoholism
and Growing Up In an Alcoholic Home

MINDCOACH FOR KIDS
Teaching Kids and Teens To Think Positive and Feel Good

WOULD YOU GIVE TWO MINUTES A DAY
FOR A LIFETIME OF LOVE?

TEN STEPS TO BUILDING VALUES WITHIN CHILDREN

A TEENAGER'S GUIDE TO A.D.D.

Confidentiality is essential to psychiatric practice. All case descriptions in this book, therefore, have been altered to preserve the anonymity of my patients without distorting the essentials of their stories.

The information offered in this book is not intended to be a substitute for the advice and counsel of your personal physician. Consult with your physician before making any medical changes.

To my father

Acknowledgments

I am grateful to the many patients and their families who have allowed me the most intimate of looks into the very function of their minds. I also send heartfelt thanks to my friends and colleagues Matthew Stubblefield, MD, Cecil Oakes, MD, Stanley Yantis, MD, Jennifer Lendl, PhD, Ronnette Leonard, MFCC, Jonathan Scott Halverstadt, MFCC and Robert Gessler, BBS who have shared cases, talked at length with me about this work and reviewed the manuscript. Also, to my research assistant Lucinda Tilley who has helped me prepare the images and proofread the text.

I also wish to thank my mother and father who are a continual source of encouragement and strength.

Contents

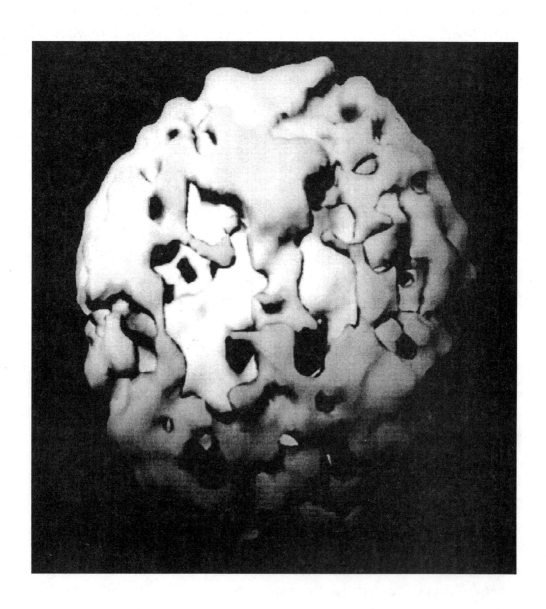

Introduction

Willie Lee Williams was the kind of guy who got along with everyone. An A student, he had a college scholarship waiting for him, and his future seemed altogether promising. Until -- his head collided with the dashboard when his car accidentally hit a guardrail. Although Willie felt dazed, he was all right. Then three months later he got into another accident when he swerved to avoid hitting a dog that had run out into the street. His head went through the windshield, and this time he had to be sent to an emergency room. After examining Willie, the doctor told him he had nothing to worry about. He only had a minor concussion. In the months that followed, however, he found that that "minor concussion" the doctor said he had, was wreaking havoc with his life. Normally a friendly person, he found himself suddenly losing his temper at the smallest things. His whole attitude and demeanor began to change before his eyes. Where he had once been patient, he now had a short fuse. Where he had once been amiable and calm, he was now constantly angry. His irritability and flares of temper were so continuous that he began to alienate his friends and family.

The brunt of his anger came to rest on his roommate and strangely began to center around food. Inexplicably, Willie's appetite was changing. In just three months, he had put on seventy pounds, and he was hungry all the time. To his roommate, Willie seemed to be devouring every morsel of food in the house. When his roommate finally got fed up and asked Willie to eat only the food he himself bought, Willie felt that by depriving him of the food he needed, he was trying to hurt him. After that comment, Willie was consumed with negative, paranoid thoughts about this person who was "trying to take the food out of his mouth." The only way to protect himself against this enemy, was to hurt the enemy. One afternoon he took a huge meat cleaver and a butcher knife and waited at the front door for the man who used to be his friend. "He was going to be instantaneously dissolved," Willie told me.

Yet even as he was gripped by paranoia lurking behind the door, some part of Willie's mind was still "sane". He saw himself, as if from above, holding these weapons, and knew he was out of control. He had to stop himself before it was too late. Immediately he rushed to the telephone and called a friend who gave him my telephone number.

Willie was involved in two minor accidents that he seemed to have simply walked away from, but he had actually suffered damage to parts of his brain, and that meant that everything he and those around him called his personality was "altered." The brain is the seat of the mind, and the mind creates the world -- a radical statement to ordinary thinking. Yet it is the mind that perceives and experiences. Everything begins and ends in the mind. How our mind works determines the very quality of life: How happy we will be, how well we will get along with others, and how successful we will be in our profession. The patterns of our mind predispose what kind of husband or wife we will be, whether we will fail in school, whether we are irritable with our children, or have the ambition to strive towards our goals.

I am a neuropsychiatrist in the San Francisco Bay Area of Northern California. Willie Williams came to see me on a Tuesday afternoon. He described for me his two accidents and the severity of his personality changes. I immediately ordered a brain study called SPECT (Single Photon Emission Computerized Tomography), which has in the last eight years revolutionized the way I practice medicine. SPECT is a nuclear medicine study that looks at brain metabolism and blood flow. It gives pictures of how well a patient's brain is functioning. As I expected, Willie's brain study was abnormal. Two areas were working too hard. One area was in his left temporal lobe, where dysfunction is often associated with paranoia and a short fuse. The second area was the top, middle section of the frontal lobes, the part of the brain that allows a person to shift attention freely from one thing to another. When that area is overactive, people get stuck in thought spirals. The minute I saw Willie's brain study it clearly explained for me the changes that had been occurring in his personality: paranoia, fiery temper, and consummation in negative thoughts about his roommate, which he couldn't turn off.

The next step was clear. I prescribed medication to alleviate his symptoms: an anti-seizure medication for the temporal lobe abnormality and an anti-obsessive antidepressant to help him get "unstuck" from negative thoughts. After several months of treatment, the results were dramatic. Willie began to regain his sense of humor and to reconnect with his friends and family. At the time of this writing, it has been five years since his two accidents. He is now gainfully employed and has even recently been promoted. He has also been blessed with a stable intimate relationship. Now on medication, he is one of the nicest human beings you will ever meet. The man who said, "I was a short fuse on a stick of dynamite," hasn't touched a meat cleaver in years.

Most of us are not on a short fuse on a stick of dynamite. We do not use meat cleavers to deal with roommates who want us to stop raiding the refrigerator. Pretty much, we just post a note under the magnet and leave it at that. Most of us are warm, kind, reasonable people who want to form meaningful relationships and be successful in our day-to-day lives. When our brain patterns are normal and balanced, we are generally able to do all these things. When behavior becomes "abnormal," however, as in Willie's case, often there is something the matter with the patterns in the body's computer -- the brain. Willie's problems may seem pronounced and unusual to us, yet fundamentally we are just like him. The actual physical patterns of our brain (which in Willie's case were disrupted) have a dramatic impact on how we think, feel and behave from moment to moment. Only recently have we discovered how to recognize those patterns and how to treat them with both behavioral and medical prescriptions.

Until recently, scientists had no sophisticated tools for evaluating a working brain. Brain MRI (Magnetic Resonance Imaging) scans and CAT (Computerized Axial Tomography) scans, available since the 1970's, are anatomy studies, and although they can evaluate what a brain physically looks like, they cannot provide information on the brain at work. EEG's (electroencephalograms) make some inroads by measuring electrical activity in the brain, but this information provides little sophisticated information into the workings of the deep structures in the brain. SPECTs, on the other hand, show what happens to the brain when you try to work it. With this tool, I and other colleagues around the country, have been able to correlate the functions of different brain parts to certain behavior in patients and see how abnormal brain patterns cause specific problems.

Many psychiatrists and neurologists, however, lack sophisticated information on how the brain actually works, and operate on theories and assumptions that are outdated. That is to say, they believe the behavior of their patients is primarily the result of early environmental conditioning, and do not consider the possibility that it may be based on abnormal brain physiology. Willie Williams, for example, could have talked to a therapist about his toilet training until the end of the millennium, and it would not have helped him. In many circles, even today, schizophrenia, manic depressive disorder, and attention deficit disorder are still blamed on bad mothering rather than a chemical or physical imbalance in the brain. In the face of a scarcity of information, smart people sometimes develop elaborate explanations for behavior that may have little or nothing to do with the truth.

In this book, as I try to help you gain a clearer understanding of the brain from which you will be able to piece together the behavior we call human, I will frequently be referring to SPECT studies because they are a form of brain imaging that is giving us essential information previously unavailable. In my own clinical practice, I have utilized SPECT studies in over 3,000 cases, and they have contributed greatly to my understanding of the brain patterns that influence specific behavior and feeling states. From the very first month I started using them I found them to be not only clinically valuable, but they changed my perception on why many people do what they do.

In the scientific world, all scientists will probably not agree with every finding I present in this book. Some of my beliefs and my enthusiasm can be accounted for by identifying a few of the advantages I have had in my practice. The Brain Imaging Division of The Amen Clinic for Behavioral Medicine, which I run, has done more brain SPECT studies for psychiatric reasons than almost any clinic in America. Experience is one of the best teachers in medicine. Two, I have had the privilege of working closely with a nuclear medicine physician, Jack Paldi, MD, who had a passion for applying his knowledge to psychiatry. (It is rare to find a psychiatrist and a nuclear medicine physician working together. While a natural connection between the specialties is not now recognized, my belief is that we will see this combination occur more and more in the next ten years.) Three, Dr. Paldi and I have had the use of one of the best SPECT cameras available which provides more and better information than the older cameras.

The purpose of this book is not to encourage readers to go out and get their brains scanned. The purpose is to help explain a wide variety of human behaviors, both aberrant and normal, by showing the images of the brain that SPECT provides. These images make it plain that many problems long thought of as psychiatric in nature -- depression, panic disorders, attention deficit disorders -- are actually medical problems that can be treated along a medical model, not just treated along the traditional psychological and sociological models.

In this book I have tried to employ the technical terms used by physicians in a "user friendly" way, and to divide the information into two distinct parts.

In Part One, The Mind and How It Functions, I show what the different parts of your brain actually do, and what happens when things go wrong. As we will see, some people suffer from actual disease or pathological states, but many more of us suffer from subclinical patterns: habits that are not crippling, yet interfere with our lives, such as constant anger, moodiness or anxiety. I describe each of the five systems of the brain, and give the behavior disorders associated with each system. I will offer new insights into a number of questions: Why do people avoid conflict? Why does divorce feel so horrible and death so disorienting? Why is casual sex bad? Why is it better not to argue with someone who is obviously stuck in a position?

In Part Two, Prescriptions for Healing the Mind, I discuss how to "fix" those areas of the brain that are over- or underactive, and how to enhance the working of specific parts that are already normal. "Prescriptions," i.e. what you can actually do to change your behavior, will be offered that will help you optimize the functioning of your brain. You might believe that a medical solution can only mean drugs, but as we will see, teaching people different ways to think can have an enormous impact on their lives. Every time you have a thought, the body releases chemicals -- that's how thinking happens -- changing thought patterns will effect brain chemistry which in turn can have an impact on all of the other cells in your body. In the prescriptions I will offer thinking and behavioral exercises, which can be effected easily in the course of everyday life. These exercises will help release you from unconscious negative patterns and abnormal brain patterns. I will also clearly spell out what medications work in each part of the brain.

The images in this book may, as they have for me, change your whole perception of why people do what they do. I maintain that human behavior is more complex than society's damning labels would have us believe. We are far too quick to attribute blame for someone's actions to bad character when the source of these actions may not be their choice at all, but a problem with the physiology of their brain. One teenage boy, for example, brought in to see me for both suicidal and violent tendencies, had a temporal lobe problem. He had a dramatic positive response to anti-seizure medication. He was not a "bad kid" after all. As he told his mother later, "I always wanted to be polite, but before this treatment my brain wouldn't let me." I often wonder how many "bad kids" sitting in reform school would prove to be perfectly nice people with the intervention of the right treatment. With this teenager, as with many of my patients over the years, I've found that seeing the dramatic changes in them, in their apparent faults, has challenged some of the basic beliefs ingrained in me as a Catholic schoolboy. Sometimes people aren't being loving, industrious, cheerful, peaceful, obedient or kind -- not because they are choosing to be a thorn in everyone's side, but because something is wrong with their brain that is potentially fixable.

Ultimately, then, I have three goals for this book:

1) That you will gain empathy and understanding for those around you whom exhibit difficult behavior and lack the tools to deal with it.

2) That the "prescriptions" I will put forward will help you change the negative patterns in your own behavior.

3) To further the national dialogue on finding effective interventions for people who suffer mental or behavioral difficulties.

Part 1

The
Mind
And
How
It
Functions

Chapter One

GETTING TO A NEW UNDERSTANDING
A Brief History

On November 8, 1895 in Wurzburg Germany, it was a dark night. Wilhelm Roentgen, a physicist at the University of Wurzburg, was working late in his laboratory. In an experiment he had been conducting before dinner, he had been sending an electric current through an evacuated tube. From a crystalline material on the other side of the lab, a light was being emitted. This made no sense to him. The cathode rays produced by the tube could only travel a few centimeters; there was no way that they could travel all the way across the room to the crystal. So where was the light from the crystal coming from? When Roentgen came back after dinner, he tried the experiment again. This time he blackened the room, blocking out all light from the windows and covering the cathode ray tube with black cardboard so no light could possibly escape when he sent another electric current through it. Yet still the crystalline material emitted visible light. Roentgen realized that it was caused by some kind of rays coming from the cathode tube that were far more penetrating than the cathode rays. Since he had never seen this phenomenon reported in the literature before and didn't know what the emitted rays were, he named them X-rays to signify their unknown nature.

Roentgen invited his wife Bertha into his lab to witness the experiment. The week before Christmas he made an X-ray of the bones in her left hand -- the first X-ray ever of the human body.

After Roentgen published a short paper on the phenomenon, the newspapers got a hold of his miracle and sensationalized it. The physicist's life was never the same again. In 1901 he won the first Nobel Prize in physics. An intensely private man, he did not relish the attention he got for his discovery. He certainly did not predict the impact his discovery would have on the lives of millions of people.

Many remarkable inventions and discoveries came out of the second half of the 19th century in science, but it would be hard to overestimate the sensation Roentgen created with his skeletal photographs and the impact of his discovery on medicine, for it provided a way to see into the body without cutting it open. It was to be many years before scientists understood the true nature of X-rays. Roentgen did not, at the time, realize that what he had done was to cause the crystal in his laboratory to emit radiation. By bombarding the atoms of the crystal with the high energy photons from the X-rays, he had knocked the electrons of the crystal's atoms out of orbit. Whenever electrons move back from a higher energy orbit into a lower energy orbit they emit photons which are what we call electromagnetic radiation. Depending on where the emission is on the electromagnetic spectrum, it will be visible or not visible to the naked eye. In Roentgen's case, the electromagnetic rays were clearly visible.

Roentgen's first paper on the subject described about 40 different properties of his newly discovered X-rays. In 1896, when another scientist, Henri Becquerel, read Roentgen's paper he noticed that these properties had a number of similarities to those he himself had observed in an unusual rock in his possession. When he first observed the rock, he did not realize it was emitting its own energy. Roentgen's paper helped him discover the principle of radiation. But where Roentgen had accidentally "created" radiation with his device, Becquerel was the first to discover the principal of radioactivity.

Marie Curie, one of Becquerel's students, found that certain of her samples of uranium had higher levels of activity than other samples. Upon investigation she discovered the reason: other elements, polonium (which gives off 700 times more radiation than uranium) and radium (which gives off a million more times more radiation than uranium) were mixed in with the uranium ore. Radium and polonium were important in that they alerted scientists to the fact that there were particles in nature that produced their own energy, as opposed to everything else on Earth, which require energy from an outside source -- the sun.

Radium was the first radioactive material ever used in medicine. However, it has an extremely long half-life. Simply for the sake of science, no one was interested in injecting a long-lived radioactive isotope into the body that was going to remain in it destroying cells for the rest of the person's life. Therefore, when the medical possibilities for radioactive substances were recognized, scientists realized they needed to find an isotope that would do the job without doing long-term or estimable damage.

In Marie Curie's day, however, they were stuck with whatever nature had made available, and the radioactive materials nature mostly made available had a half-life that lasted many, many years. It was important to scientists to be able to artificially produce radioactive substances with properties that allowed them to be used in the human body. In other words, they needed radioisotopes that would do whatever they were supposed to do and then disappear. Irene Curie (Marie's daughter) recognized this and found a way to artificially create radioactive material. (Eventually technetium, which proved to be a very good short-acting isotope, was discovered and is still used today.) Of course, they could not possibly have known how to produce mass quantities of radioisotopes at the turn of the century. It was not until World War II, after the Manhattan Project developed the atomic bomb, that science was able to achieve that. The experimental nuclear reactor furnished a rich source of neutrons that generated radioisotopes in large quantities for a low cost. From then on, there was no scarcity of radioactive material, either for national defense or for medicine.

Many other important discoveries along the way helped nuclear medicine get where it is today. As early as 1903, Alexander Graham Bell suggested the first clinical use of radioactive material. In a letter he stated the possibility of using radium in a sealed glass tube which could be inserted near a tumor in a patient. On of the most important discoveries, however, was made in 1927 by Herman Blumgart and his colleagues in Boston when using a diluted solution of radon to study circulation. By measuring how fast blood got from one side of the body to the other, they were able to measure circulation and cardiac functions. Consequently they were the first to use radioactive isotopes to measure physiological functions in the body, and their discovery ushered in the "nuclear age" of medicine. It was Dr. Blumgart's and other studies conducted in the 1920s observing the transportation of radioactive elements in the body that lead to the conclusion that radioactive material could be used as a tracer. The "nuclear age" of medicine has been of immense importance to people suffering from disease and injury because it has created new and safer ways for doctors to diagnose what is wrong with them.

What is SPECT? SPECT stands for Single Photon Emission Computerized Tomography. It is a sophisticated nuclear medicine study that looks at brain activity (or metabolism) and blood flow. In this study, a radioactive isotope (which, as we will see, is akin to a beacon of energy) is connected to a substance (like HMPAO -- hexamethyl propylamine oxine) with properties that make it readily taken up by the brain. This compound is then injected into the patient's vein where it runs throughout the blood stream and locks into certain receptor sites in the brain. A SPECT camera is used to detect where the compound (signaled by the radioisotope acting like a beacon of light) has gone. It takes a supercomputer to then reconstruct the 3-D snapshots of the brain. Each 14-16 minute exposure the camera takes colorizes brain activity, allowing physicians to see specific patterns. The elegant snapshots that result then offer us a sophisticated blood flow/metabolism map. With these maps, physicians have been able to identify certain brain patterns that correlate with psychiatric and neurological illnesses.

SPECT studies belong to a branch of medicine called nuclear medicine. Nuclear (which refers to the nucleus of an atom) medicine must use radioactive material because it is made up of unstable atoms which we make use of in the following way. An unstable atom is always looking for stability, and it will keep changing, degrading, until it reaches its most stable form. At each step of decay, it emits portions of energy. Scientists can use that energy because they can follow it in the same way you would follow a boat afloat at sea if somebody aboard has a flashlight; you would simply track the flashlight beam. Thus an unstable atom is essentially a tracking device.

Nuclear medicine studies measure the physiological functioning of the body, and they can be used to diagnose a multitude of medical conditions: heart disease, certain forms of infection, the spread of cancer, and bone and thyroid disease. My own branch of nuclear medicine, the brain, uses SPECT studies to help in the diagnosis of schizophrenia, dementia, mood disorders, stroke, seizures, and head trauma.

SPECTs are not the only diagnostic tool in the physician's arsenal. In the late 1970's and early 80's CAT scans and MRIs became very popular. Physicians were able to see tumors, strokes, and blood clots in the exquisite images. The resolution of those images was so superior to the nuclear medicine brain studies, in fact, that they nearly eliminated their use altogether. Yet despite their clarity, CAT scans and MRIs could only offer images of a static brain, of the brain's anatomy; they gave little or no information on a working brain. In the last decade it has become increasingly recognized that many neurological and psychiatric disorders are not disorders of the brain's anatomy, but problems in how it functions.

Two technological advancements have begun to encourage the use, once again, of SPECT studies. Initially, the SPECT cameras were single-headed, and they took a long time to scan a person's brain (up to an hour). People had trouble holding still that long, and the images were fuzzy, hard to read (earning nuclear medicine the nickname "unclear medicine") and they did not give much information about the functioning deep in the brain. Then multi-headed cameras were developed which were able to image the brain much faster. The advancement of computer technology allowed for improved data acquisition from the multi-headed systems. The brain SPECT studies of today, with their higher resolution, can see into the deeper areas of the brain with far greater clarity and show what CAT scans and MRIs cannot – show how the brain actually functions.

SPECT studies can be displayed in a variety of different ways. Traditionally, the brain is examined in three different planes: horizontally (cut from top to bottom), coronally (cut from front to back), and sagittally (cut from side to side). What do physicians see when they look at a SPECT study? We examine it for shades of color (in different color scales depending on the physician's preference, including gray scales) and pattern and compare it to what we know a normal brain looks like. The color images that accompany this book will appear in a spectrum from red at the high end to orange, yellow, and finally blue and black at the low end. In this color scale red indicates the highest activity, blue and black the least amount of activity. In a normal brain the overall color tends to be orange/red, with some yellow, and blue. Generally speaking, the occipital cortex/cerebellum (at the back bottom portion of the brain) is the hottest, or the most red. Throughout the text, gray scale images will appear. Physicians are usually alerted that something is wrong in one of three ways: (a) they see too much red, meaning a part of the brain is overactive; (b) they see too much blue or black, meaning that a part of the brain is underactive; or (c) they see colors on each side of the image that are asymmetrical which ought to be symmetrical.

VIEWING BRAIN SPECT STUDIES

HORIZONTAL VIEW (transaxial)
The brain is viewed in horizontal slices, cut from top to bottom.
It is as if you are looking down from a bird's eye view.

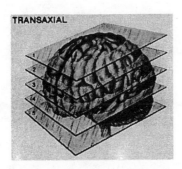

CORONAL VIEW (front on view)
The brain is viewed in vertical slices, cut from front to back.
It is as if you are looking face on or front on to the brain.

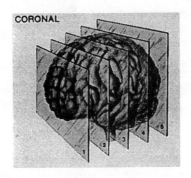

SAGITTAL VIEW (side to side)
The brain is viewed in vertical slices, cut from side to side.
It is as if you are looking at the brain from the side.

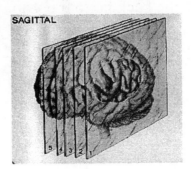

Normal Brain SPECT Studies

front

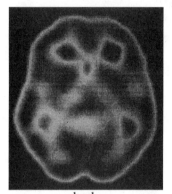

back

normal horizontal view

top

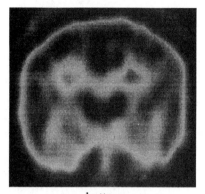

bottom

normal coronal view

top

front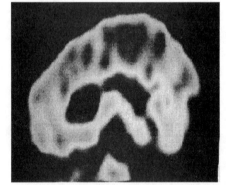

bottom

normal sagittal (side) view

back

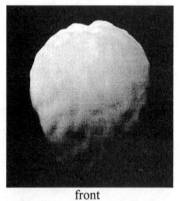

front

normal 3-D surface view, looking down on brain

front

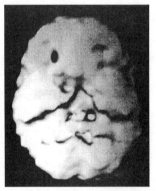

back

normal 3-D undersurface view
looking up from the bottom

back

front

normal 3-dimensional view looking down
from the top, gray equals average activity,
white equals the hottest 13% of the brain,
back of the brain is normally the most active

In the rest of the book, I will go into greater detail about how this remarkable technology has touched people's lives. For right now, however, I will simply offer a sample of six common ways in which SPECT studies are utilized in medicine.

1. To make early intervention possible. Ellen was a 63-year-old woman who experienced a sudden onset of paralysis on the right side of her body. Unable to even speak, she was in a panic and her family was extremely concerned. As drastic as these symptoms were, two hours after the event, her CAT scan was still normal. Suspecting a stroke, the emergency room physician ordered a brain SPECT study which showed a hole of activity where a blood vessel had broken and was choking off the blood supply to the brain. This was causing brain tissue death in the left front part. From this information, it was clear that a stroke was evolving and her doctors were able to take measures to limit the extent of the damage.

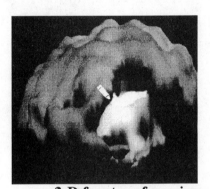

3-D front surface view
notice the large hole which
indicates a left frontal lobe stroke

2. To evaluate the patient accurately so that future illness can be prevented. Nancy was a 59-year-old woman suffering from severe depression that had been nonresponsive to treatment. Upon admission to a psychiatric hospital a SPECT study was done to evaluate her condition. Since she had not experienced any symptoms that would point to this, I was surprised to see that she had had two large strokes. Nearly immediately her non-responsive depression had made more sense to me. Sixty percent of the people who have frontal lobe strokes experience severe depression. As a result of the SPECT study, I sought immediate consultation with a neurologist who evaluated her for the possible causes of the stroke, such as plaques in the arteries of the neck or abnormal heart rhythms. He

felt the stroke had come from a blood clot and placed her on blood thinning medication to prevent further strokes.

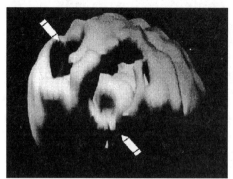

3-D side surface view
notice the 2 large holes which
indicate 2 right brain strokes

3. To help the physician elicit understanding and compassion from the patient's family. When Frank, a wealthy, well-educated man, entered his seventies, he began to grow forgetful. At first it was over small things, but as time went on the lapses of memory progressed to the point where he often forgot essential facts of his life: where he lived, his wife's name and even his own name. His wife and children, not understanding the change in behavior, were aggravated with his absent-mindedness and often angry at him for it. Frank's SPECT study showed a marked suppression across the entire brain, but especially in the frontal lobes and the parietal and temporal lobes. From long experience, I knew this was a classic Alzheimer's disease pattern. By showing the family these images and pointing out the physiological cause of Frank's forgetfulness, in living color so to speak, I helped them understand that he was not trying to be annoying, but had a serious medical problem.

Consequently, instead of blaming him for his memory lapses, they began to show compassion towards him, and they developed strategies to deal more effectively with the problems of living with a person who has Alzheimer's Disease. In addition, I placed Frank on new experimental treatments for Alzheimer's Disease.

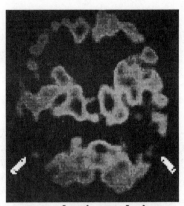

horizontal view
Alzheimer's Disease
marked suppression

4.   To differentiate from one another two problems with similar symptoms. I first met Margaret when she was 68 years old. Her appearance was ragged and unkempt. She lived alone and her family was worried about her because she appeared to have symptoms of serious dementia. They finally admitted her to the psychiatric hospital where I worked after she had gone out to perform an errand one day and left a burner on the stove, nearly burning her own house down. When I consulted with the family I also found out that Margaret often forgot the names of her own children and frequently got lost when driving her car. Her driving habits deteriorated to the point where the Department of Motor Vehicles (DMV) had to take away her license after four minor accidents in a six-month period. At the time when Margaret's family saw me, some members had had enough and were ready to put her into a board and care home. Some, however, were against the idea and wanted her hospitalized for further evaluation.

    While at first glance it may have appeared that Margaret was suffering from Alzheimer's Disease, the results of her SPECT study showed full activity in her frontal, parietal and temporal lobes. If she had had Alzheimer's Disease, there should have been evidence of decreased blood flow in those areas. Instead, the only abnormal activity shown on Margaret's SPECT was in the limbic system at the center of the brain where the activity was increased. Often, this is a findingin patients suffering from clinical depres-sion. It can be difficult to distinguish between Alzheimer's Disease and pseudodementias because the symptoms in the elderly can be similar. Yet with pseudodementia, a person may appear demented yet not be at all; the symptoms are caused by other factors such as, as in this case, serious depression. This is an important distinction to make because a diagnosis of Alzheimer's Disease would lead to prescribing a set of coping strategies to the family and possibly new experimental medications, whereas a diagnosis of some form of depression would lead to prescribing an aggressive treatment of antidepressant medication for the patient along with psychotherapy.

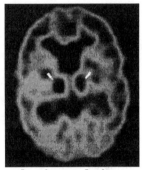 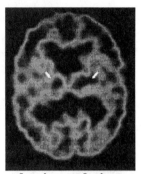

horizontal view
before treatment

horizontal view
after treatment

Notice good cortical (surface) activity, with increased limbic system
activity at rest which improves or normalizes after treatment with buprion.

The results of Margaret's SPECT study convinced me to have her try the antidepressant Wellbutrin. After three weeks, I and other staff members noticed that she was talkative, well-groomed, and was not isolating herself from the other patients. After a month in the hospital she was released to go home. Before discharge she asked me if I would write a letter to the DMV to help her get her driver's license back. Since I drive on the same highways as her I was a bit hesitant. I told her that if in six months she remained improved I would write to the DMV for her. Six months later she remained markedly improved. I repeated her SPECT study. It was completely normal. I wrote the letter to the DMV and they gave her back her license!

5. To discern when a problem is the result of abuse and remove the patient from a dangerous environment. Betty was the most beautiful 88-year-old woman I had ever met. She was very proper and very proud. When she was a young woman she had emigrated from England to this country after marrying a U.S. soldier. It was not her 90-year-old husband who brought her to the hospital to see me, however, it was her sister. Her husband, far from being supportive, angrily denied that his wife was suffering from serious cognitive problems. Yet during the

evaluation process it was clear that Betty had severe memory problems; she did not know where she lived, her phone number, or her husband's name. I ordered a SPECT study that showed a dent in the right side of Betty's frontal lobe. It was obvious to me that she had, at some point in her life, suffered a significant head injury. When I asked her about it, all she could do was look down and cry; she could not give me details of the event. When I asked her sister, she reported that Betty and her husband had had a stormy relationship and that he was abusive towards her. He would sometimes grab her by the hair and slam her head into the wall. The sister wanted Betty to go to the police, but Betty said it would only make things worse.

Shortly after Betty was hospitalized, her husband began pressuring me to send her home. He kept protesting that there was nothing wrong with her, yet I knew that Betty needed to be removed from that environment so I contacted the Adult Protective Services. At Betty's hearing, I used her SPECT studies to convince the judge that her home held potential danger. He then ordered her to have a conservator, and she went to live with her sister.

3-D front surface view
notice the areas of decreased
activity in the right frontal cortex

6. Help in the diagnosis and treatment of unresponsive conditions complicated by drug abuse. Twenty-eight-year-old Rusty was brought to see me by his parents. He had a severe methamphetamine problem that had wreaked havoc in his life. He was unable to keep steady work, he was involved in a physically abusive relationship with his girlfriend (arrested four times for assault and battery), he was mean to his parents even though they tried to help him, and he had failed five drug

treatment programs. In the last drug treatment program the counselor recommended a "tough love" approach. He told the parents to make Rusty hit bottom so that he would want help. The parents read about my work and decided to do one more thing before going the "tough love" route. Initially, I wanted to scan Rusty. His lack of responsiveness to traditional treatments made me suspect an underlying brain problem, but he had no insurance to pay for the scan. I tried several medications and counseling approaches without success. I then convinced the parents to get the scan. In the long run I felt it would actually save us money in Rusty's treatment. The SPECT was scheduled with the parents, but Rusty did not know that the scan was scheduled until the morning he was supposed to have it. He showed up at the clinic loaded on high dose methamphetamine from the night before. Always honest with me, Rusty told me about his drug abuse. He said, "I'm sorry for messing up the scan. I'll come back next week. I promise I won't use anything." I had often wanted to do SPECT studies on people intoxicated with illegal substances to see their effects on the brain. But due to ethical reasons I had not been able to. I decided to scan Rusty that morning with the effects of the methamphetamine still in his system and then a week later off all drugs. To my amazement it turned out to be a very fortuitous decision. When Rusty was under the influence of high dose methamphetamine his brain looked suppressed in activity. A week later, however, off all drugs, he had a terribly hot or overactive left temporal lobe. As we will see, left temporal lobe problems often correlate with violence. Rusty was self-medicating an underlying temporal lobe problem with high dose methamphetamine. As I probed deeper into any history of a head injury, which initially both Rusty and his parents denied, Rusty remembered a time when he was in second grade where he ran full speed into a solid metal basketball pole and was briefly knocked unconscious. That could have caused his temporal lobe problem. Given this finding, I put Rusty on Tegretol (an anti-seizure medication which stabilizes activity in the temporal lobes). Within 2 weeks Rusty felt better than he had in years. He was calmer, his temper was under control and for the first time in his life he was able to remain gainfully employed. An additional benefit of the scan was that I showed Rusty the serious damage he was doing to his brain by abusing the methamphetamines. Even though the drugs helped his temporal lobe problem, they were clearly toxic to his brain. Rusty, like others who abuse drugs, developed holes of brain activity across the surface of his brain. Seeing these pictures was even more incentive to stay away from the drugs and get proper treatment for his problems. I wonder how many people with severe non-responsive drug problems are self-medicating an underlying problem, yet are labeled by their families and society in general as weak willed or morally defective?

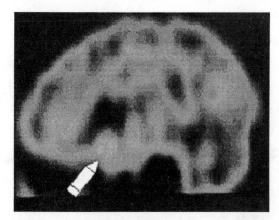

side view
on high dose methamphetamine

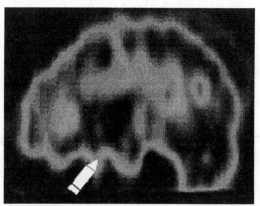

side view
off methamphetamine

** while on high dose drug the left temporal lobe appears relatively normal
** when off drug there is marked increased activity in the left temporal lobe

3-D surface view
looking down from the top
notice multiple areas of decreased activity

7. Help in the understanding and education about serious drug abuse. Robert, age 39, came to see me because he thought he had attention deficit disorder. He was forgetful, disorganized, impulsive and he had a very short attention span.

However, he did not have these problems in school growing up. They came on gradually during his adult life. Most notably, he also had a 20-year history of heroin abuse and he had been in multiple treatment settings. It is hard to describe my own personal feelings when I initially saw his SPECT study. This man was about my age, yet through abusing drugs his brain took on the functional pattern of someone 50 years older who had a dementia-like process.

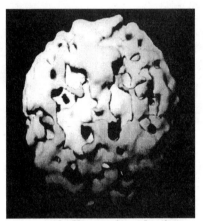

3-dimensional view
looking down from the top
notice the large holes of activity across the brain surface

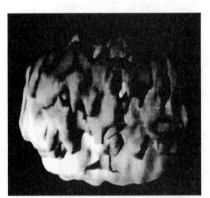

3-dimensional view
front underside of brain
notice marked decreased activity across the brain surface

When I showed Robert his SPECT study he was horrified. Even though he tried to stop abusing heroin on multiple occasions this time he went into treatment and was able to stop. Later he told me, "It was either the heroin or my brain. I wasn't giving any more of my brain to the drug."

Researchers are consistently finding that the effects of drug and alcohol abuse can cause serious damage to the brain. I often show Robert's pictures to the teenagers I see in my office, as well as to groups of teenagers when I lecture around the country. I find them more powerful than looking at fried eggs.

****

It will be clear from these, and many other stories in this book, that a doctor who can give an accurate diagnosis can be the greatest friend a patient can have. By now, you may be starting to have an understanding as to why this technology has so forcefully grabbed my attention.

Chapter Two

IMAGES OF MOOD
The Limbic System

Functions

- sets the emotional tone of the mind
- stores highly charged emotional memories
- alters moods and emotions
- modulates motivation
- affects bonding and social connectedness
- controls sleep and appetite cycles
- processes directly the sense of smell
- modulates the libido

The limbic system is in the subcortical area at the center of the brain. Considering it's size -- about that of a walnut -- it is power-packed with functions, all of which are critical for human behavior.

This is the part of the brain that sets a person's emotional tone and stores highly charged emotional memories, both positive and negative. If you have been traumatized by a dramatic event, like being in an automobile accident or watching your house burn down, or if you have been abused by a parent or a spouse for instance, the memory is stored in the limbic system of the brain. On the other hand, if you have won the lottery, graduated magna cum laude from Harvard, or watched your child be born, that is stored there too. Memory, in relationships, can either work for or against you. Positive memories can enhance the bond between two people, and negative memories can drive a wedge between them. The following are two case scenarios.

Ann and Phillip had a good marriage for most of their fourteen years. When it began to go sour, they first consulted their pastor, who then sent them to me. The crux of their fights was over the fact that Phillip had had an affair with

Ann's best friend who was going through a divorce. Ann felt hurt and betrayed, yet through counseling she was able to forgive Phillip. Understanding the reasons for the affair helped. Yet, more important than understanding, for Ann, was the fact that she had had many happy memories to draw upon from years of good times with her husband. They helped her heal the wounds and gave her a solid base for wanting to save the marriage. Recalling positive memories helped Ann get in touch with all the reasons she had married Phillip in the first place.

Marie and Steve were another story. Their relationship had been beset by fighting from the very beginning. To make matters worse, Marie was pregnant at the time that they got married, so they had never had a chance to work out their difficulties and bond together as a couple before taking on the responsibilities of a child. Consequently, when Steve caught Marie having an affair, he did not work at holding the marriage together. With only negative memories to fall back on, he didn't feet there was anything to fight for. He simply packed his bags, left the house, and filed for divorce within a month.

The limbic system also affects motivation and drive. It helps get you going in the morning and encourages you to move throughout the day. It controls the sleep and appetite cycles of the body. It affects the bonding mechanism which enables you to connect with other people on a social level; your ability to do this successfully in turn influences your moods. Humans are not like polar bears, wandering the tundra alone eleven months out of the year. We are social animals. When we are bonded to people in a positive way, we feel better about ourselves and our lives. This capacity to bond then plays a significant role in the tone and quality of our moods.

Another way in which the limbic system has a bearing upon our moods is the way it affects the libido, the sexual drive. When the limbic system is overactive, a general depression can result that makes people lose interest in sex. The obverse is also true: for a person who is not connecting with another in a sexual way the energy of the limbic system may be continually increasing, meaning that the depression is continually fed. Whenever a person is sexually involved with another, neurochemical changes occur in both their brains which encourage limbic bonding. Limbic bonding is the reason casual sex doesn't really work for people on a whole mind and body level. Two people may decide to have sex "just for the fun of it," yet something is occurring on another level they might not have decided on at all: Sex is enhancing an emotional bond between them whether they want it or not. One person, often the woman, is bound to form an attachment and will get hurt when the affair ends. The reason it is usually the woman is that the size of a woman's limbic system, in comparison to the rest of her body, is larger than it is for a man. Consequently, she is more likely to get limbically connected.

I once had a patient named Renee who had a high sex drive, which was not getting satisfied by her husband. For years other men flirted with her and she remained faithful, until one day she decided, out of pure frustration, to have an affair with a co-worker. From the outset, they agreed that they were going to have friendly sex, just for fun, just for the pleasure, and in the first two months that seemed to work. Then Renee felt herself wanting to see him more often. She tried to get him to meet with her twice a week instead of once a week. Instead of responding positively, her lover pulled away, and so it went along like that. The more attached she became, the more detached he became. Although Renee and her lover had been on the same wavelength in the beginning, in the end she had changed and he hadn't, and she felt used. It is important to understand how your body and psyche work. In this case, Renee would have been wise to realize that her limbic system was not quite as open to casual sex as she wanted to be. She would have been better off to stay with her husband and work things out sexually with him, rather than to pick a casual acquaintance to have a sexual liaison with.

The limbic system also contains the powerful pleasure and pain centers of the brain, and we all know how much physical and emotional suffering can alter our moods. Again there is a circular effect because when one is depressed, pain -- any physical suffering -- can be felt more acutely than at other times, and pleasure, when it does come one's way, is more likely to be overlooked.

The limbic system directly processes your sense of smell. The olfactory sense is the only one of the five senses that is directly processed in this part of the brain. The messages from all the other senses (sight, hearing, touch and taste) are processed in a "way station," the thalamus, before they are sent to their final destination in different parts of the brain. Because your sense of smell goes directly to the limbic system, which happens to control the emotions, it is easy to see why smells can have such a powerful impact on our feeling states. The multibillion-dollar perfume and deodorant industries count on this fact: beautiful smells evoke pleasant feelings and draw people towards you whereas unpleasant smells cause people to withdraw. Expensive perfumes and colognes can make you beautiful, sexy and attractive to others, whereas a disagreeable body odor can make the other person wan to rush to the far side of the room. I learned about the limbic phenomenon firsthand when I was sixteen years old and dating the woman who is now my wife. She was a good Catholic girl and as a typical hot-blooded teenager I was more interested in affection than she was. One night I had accidentally run out of my cologne, so I borrowed my brother's English Leather Cologne. When I picked her up for our date I noticed a difference. She wasmore cuddly. She even took my hand before I reached for hers and came close to me before I moved toward her. Needless to say, from then on that was the only scent I wore.

Problems

- moodiness, irritability, clinical depression
- increased negative thinking
- decreased motivation
- flood of negative emotions
- sleep and appetite problems
- social isolation and withdrawal
- decreased or increased sexual responsiveness

The problems in the limbic system, as well as in all systems, correspond with their functions. Do you know people who see every situation in a bad light? That actually could be a limbic system problem because the system tends to set our emotional filter, and when it is working too hard the filter is permeated by negativity. One person could walk away from an interaction that ten others would have labeled as positive, but which he or she would consider negative. And since the limbic system affects motivation, people sometimes develop an "I don't care" attitude about life and work; they don't have the energy to care. Because they feel hopeless about the outcome, they have little willpower to follow through with tasks.

Since the sleep and appetite centers are in the limbic system, disruption can lead to changes, which may mean an inclination one way or the other, too much or too little of either. For example, in typical depressive episodes people have been known to lose their appetites and to have trouble sleeping despite being chronically tired, and yet in atypical depression they will sleep and eat excessively.

There are three problems caused by abnormalities to the limbic system that warrant their own sections: bonding disruption, affective disorders and PMS.

Bonding Disruption

Bonding problems can actually be caused by depression which, as we will see, is a function of the limbic system. People who are depressed often do not like being around others. Consequently, they isolate themselves. The social isolation tends to perpetuate itself because the more isolated a person becomes, the less bonding activity occurs, thus worsening the depression and increasing the likelihood of further isolation.

One of the most fundamental bonds in the human universe is the mother-infant bond. Hormonal changes shortly after childbirth, however, can cause emotional problems in the mother; they are called the "baby blues" when they are mild or postpartum depression or psychosis when they are severe. When this happens, the limbic system of the mother's brain shows abnormal activity. (The phenomenon has been found to occur in animals as well as humans) In turn, significant bonding problems may occur. The mother may emotionally withdraw from the baby, preventing the baby from developing normally. Babies who experience "failure-to-thrive," for instance, or who have low weight or delayed development, often have mothers who are unattached emotionally.

In the case above; it is the abnormal activity of the mother's limbic system that causes developmental problems for the baby. Conversely, problems to the limbic system can be caused by outside events that disrupt the human bonding process. This can occur at any stage in life. Here are three of the most common:

Death. The death of a parent, spouse or child causes intense sadness and grief. In these familial relationships there is often a tight neurochemical bond (from the myriad of stored memories and experiences) and when it is broken the activity of the limbic system is disrupted. Many who experience grief say the pain actually feels physical. They are not imagining it. Grief often activates the pain centers in the brain, which as we have seen, are housed in the limbic system.

It is interesting to note that the people who had a good relationship with the person who died often heal their grief much easier than those whose relationship with the deceased was filled with turmoil, bitterness or disappointment. The reason is that a positive relationship leaves behind good memories, and remembering and reprocessing good memories helps in the healing process. When people who leave behind a bad relationship think back on it, they have to relieve the pain. In their mind, they are still trying to fix what was wrong, to heal the wound, but they can't. In addition, the guilt they carry with them impairs the healing process. Donna S. is a case in point. Donna and her mother had had a stormy relationship, fighting constantly over things that seemed insignificant. Yet in spite of their problems, the year after her mother's death was the hardest of Donna's life. Her husband could not understand the force of her grief; all he ever heard her do was complain that her mother was selfish and uninterested in her. What he failed to understand was that Donna not only had to grieve over her mother's death, but also over the fact that now she would never have that mother-daughter bond she had always wanted. Death was so final and had ended all her hopes.

Losing a spouse or lover is traumatic in a different way than losing any other type of loved one. Once you have made love with a person, having the connection broken through death can be extraordinarily painful because there is a "limbic connection." The spouse has become part of the chemical bond of that part of the brain and it takes time for that bond to dissolve. Your limbic system misses the person's touch, voice and smell.

Divorce. Divorce can be a source of the most severe kind of stress it is possible for a human being to experience. For many it actually causes more anguish to lose a spouse through divorce than it does through death. As stated above, people who are "limbically connected" have a very powerful bond, and I believe this phenomenon may be one of the major reasons women cannot leave abusive men. They have had their children with these men, shared their beds and their homes with them. To break that bond, which is at the core of their brain, causes a severe rupture that can make the woman feel fragmented, as if she were not quite whole without the man. She may be plagued by sleep and appetite problems, depression, irritability and social isolation. I once treated a woman who was married to a controlling, angry man whom she could never please. On the day he told her he was leaving her for another woman (a severe limbic injury) she became so depressed that she put her head in the oven and turned on the gas. Fortunately, she was rescued and brought to the hospital. It wasn't until her limbic system began to heal and she could feel her own autonomy that she realized she didn't even like her husband, and in any case, it certainly wasn't worth killing herself over a man who cheated on her.

Even the one who initiates a separation suffers distress and often goes through a period of depression, because the "chemical limbic bonds" break for everyone involved in the separation. The one who is walking out the door may fail to realize this and not anticipate the grief period that will most certainly follow. For some, divorce is so devastating that it can trigger enormous anger and vengefulness. In fact, I have never seen two people more cruel to each other than those going through a messy divorce. They lose all sense of fairness and rationality and do everything possible to hurt one another. What ignites such passionate responses? Breaking the chemical connection activates the limbic system. People become not only depressed and negative,but oversensitive, taking every little thing the wrong way. Anger quickly follows and aggression. They know they have to separate and unconsciously they use the anger and aggression as a way to do it.

The Empty Nest Syndrome. When children leave home, parents often feel intensely sad and bereft. Many loose their appetites and have trouble sleeping. Something is missing. This may be confusing because the parents remember how arduous it was struggling through the growing pains of their offspring's' adolescence, and they assumed it would be a relief when the teenagers were finally out of the house and off to their own lives. (It has been suggested that the discordant nature of the parent-child relationship during adolescence may be nature's way of helping parents and teens make the transition from the close bond of childhood to the total independence of young adulthood.) Yet no matter how difficult those adolescent years were for both sides, a tremendous bond still exists, and breaking it is stressful.

Depression

Depression is known to be caused by a deficit of certain neuro-chemicals or neurotransmitters: especially norepinephrine and serotonin. In my experience, this deficit can cause increased metabolism or inflammation in the limbic system, which in turn causes all the problems associated with depression. You may have noticed in this chapter how, along with all the other symptoms of limbic system disruption, depression seems to be a constant factor throughout. Because the limbic system is intimately tied to moods, to how you feel, when it is overactive the ensuing problems with depression snowball and affect all the other limbic system functions.

The following SPECT study is of a woman named Ariel. She came to see me because she had been experiencing symptoms of depression for over two years. She was tired, suffered from sleeplessness and negative thinking, had no motivation, and for the first time in her life she had begun to have suicidal thoughts. The symptom that was most difficult for her husband, however, was her complete loss of interest in sex. He was ready to leave her because he thought she wasn't interested in him anymore as a man. Why else, he thought, had it been such a long time since she had wanted to touch him?

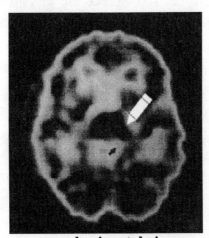

horizontal view
notice increase activity in limbic area (arrow)

After I had her brain scanned, I was not surprised to find that her limbic system was on double time. Giving this information to her husband was a powerful tool in helping him to view the situation objectively instead of subjectively as he had been. His wife was not neglecting him because she didn't like him, but because something was off-balance in the chemistry of her brain. Most important of all, the problem was rectifiable.

Increased activity in the limbic system is part of a pattern that is often responsive to antidepressants, but sometimes people are averse to being put on medication. Ariel was in such a category. She had gotten caught up in the media blitz of 1991 when the pet hair-raising topic of the news and the talk shows was that Prozac was a dangerous drug that could cause criminally aberrant behavior. It was even reported that it could cause you to kill your mother! I believe this sensationalism to have been completely irresponsible on the part of the media because it scared many people who suffered with depression, a very treatable illness, from seeking the help they needed. The fact that medication can cause side effects should not be a blanket deterrent against this form of treatment; in many, many cases, the pluses far outweigh the minuses. If you are skeptical of this statement, consider the following fact: People on antidepressants may experience constipation or an upset stomach, but suicide (often the result from untreated depression) is the ninth leading cause of death in the United States.

Ariel was persistent in her decision not to use medication. Since she wasn't suicidal, I felt safe in deferring to her preferences and offering her my "limbic prescriptions" (behavioral changes that effect the chemistry of the brain) instead of pharmaceutical prescriptions. The ones I gave her were specifically developed to treat depression. Fortunately for Ariel they were successful in bringing her out of her depressed state; however, these nonmedication prescriptions do not work for everyone and often medication is essential.

Another case that came to my attention is that of Leigh Anne. She came to see me fifteen months after the birth of her first child. Her story, as she relayed it to me, was that several weeks after her child was born she began experiencing symptoms of nausea, social withdrawal, crying spells and depression. Three months later she sought help through psychotherapy, but her condition did not improve. Her depression then progressed to the point where she became unable to care for her daughter on a day-to-day basis. Desperate to function as the good mother she wanted to be to her child, she came to see me. After diagnosing her with major depression I placed her on Prozac and began seeing her in psychotherapy. Her symptoms remitted after only several weeks. After several months Leigh Anne discontinued treat-ment. She associated taking Prozac with a course of action for "a depressed person." She did not want to see herself in that light or be stigmatized with that label. For several months after stopping she had no adverse reaction. Then the symptoms returned.

When she came to see me again Leigh Anne still didn't want to believe that anything was "wrong" with her, so she was still resistant to going back on medication. After I ordered a SPECT study to evaluate her limbic system, I was able to point out to her the marked increase in activity in that area of her brain. It provided me with the evidence needed to convince her to go back on Prozac for a while longer.

This case illustrates an important point. It has been my experience as well as that of many other psychiatrists that a patient does not necessarily have to stay on medication forever just because they have started it. However, with certain medications, like Prozac, a minimum period of treatment is necessary before it can successfully be terminated. If a depressed patient is willing to stay on their medication for long enough, about two years in this case, there is a greater chance that they can get off of it in a timely manner yet still remain free from their symptoms.

Manic-Depressive Disorder

Sarah was fifty-three years old when she was admitted to the hospital under my care. Recently, her family had her committed to another psychiatric hospital for delusional thinking and bizarre behavior -- she had actually ripped out all the electrical wiring in her home because she heard voices coming from the walls. In addition to the above symptoms, she was barely getting any sleep, her thoughts raced wildly, and she was irritable. In the previous hospital her doctor had diagnosed her with manic-depressive disorder (a potentially severe cyclical mood disorder). He had placed her on Lithium (an anti-manic medication) and Klonopin (an anti-anxiety medication). After responding well, she was sent home. But Sarah, like Leigh Anne, did not want to believe that anything was wrong with her and she stopped taking both medications. Her position was actually fortified by some members of her family who openly told her she didn't need pills, that doctors only prescribe them to force patients into numerous follow-up visits. Yet their advice was ill advised, for within weeks of stopping the treatment, Sarah's bizarre behavior returned. This was when her family brought her to the hospital where I worked. When I first saw Sarah, she was extremely paranoid. Believing that everyone was trying to hurt her, she was always looking for ways to escape the hospital. Again her thoughts were delusional; she believed she had special powers and that others were trying to take them from her. At times, she also appeared very "spacy." In an attempt to understand what was going on with her for myself, and to convince her that her problems were biological, I ordered a SPECT study.

Carrying this out did not prove easy. Our nuclear medicine clinic tried to scan her on three separate occasions. The first two times she ripped out the intravenous line saying we were trying to poison her. The third time was a success because her sister went with her and calmed her down by talking her through the experience. While the study revealed an overall increase in activity in the limbic system, I found more intensity on the left side of her scan and a marked patchy uptake across the cortex. In other words, some areas showed increased activity and some showed decreased. My experience told me that cyclic mood disorders often correlate with focal areas of increased activity in the limbic system specifically as well as a patchy uptake across the surface of the brain in general.

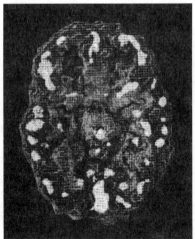

3-dimensional view looking down from the top
gray equals average activity, white equals the hottest 13% of the brain,
notice the multiple areas of increased activity across the brain

For Sarah's family, this was powerful evidence that her problems were biological, so that when she still refused medication, they were now willing to encourage her to go back on it. After she took their advice, her behavior normalized again and once I knew she was feeling better, more in control, I showed her the SPECT studies. Through a better understanding of the problem she was able to agree to follow-up visits and to stay on her medication until both she and I concurred that she could stop.

Often it is important to rescan a patient several months after the first time to see what difference the medication has made on the physiology of his or her brain. Although Sarah's new study showed a vast improvement from her earlier one, I still noticed an area of increased activity in the left temporal lobe, and Sarah was still complaining of symptoms of spaciness. I changed her medication to Depakote, which is usually used as an anti-seizure medication but can also be used for manic-depressive disorder. Not only did her psychotic symptoms remain in remission after this but the spaciness disappeared also. It is now four years later and I am happy to say that only a small dose of Depakote has given Sarah a normal life.

Sarah's case illustrates one of the most clinically significant problems in people diagnosed with manic-depressive illness. This disorder is usually quite responsive to medication. The problem is that when people afflicted by the disorder improve, they feel so normal they do not believe they ever had a chronic problem to begin with. It is difficult for people to accept that they have to keep taking medication when they think they no longer have a problem. Yet, as we have seen, prematurely stopping medication actually increases their chances for relapse. In this chapter, I have attempted to show the role SPECT studies have played in helping me address this problem. Through the use of these studies I have been able to decrease the relapse rate of my patients by demonstrating graphically the biological nature of their disorder and the need to treat it as such. It has been a great asset to me in getting patients to cooperate in their own healing process. In addition to that, it has helped me with one other important thing: to convince patient's to stop blaming themselves for their symptoms.

PMS

Cyclic mood changes associated with hormonal shifts in women are commonly known as PMS, or premenstrual syndrome. The limbic system itself has a higher density of estrogen receptors than other sections of the brain and this makes it more vulnerable, in some women, to the estrogen changes that originate in the pituitary gland and ovaries. Sometimes these changes can produce dramatic effects.

On three separate occasions Sherrie, a 35-year old nurse, left her husband. Each time, it happened within the ten days before the onset of her menstrual period. The last time she left him, her behavior escalated and she had attacked him with a knife. When I first met Sherrie, it was in the early part of her cycle, which was the good part. She appeared to be gentle and soft-spoken. It was hard to fathom that this woman who was a picture of gentility had, only days before, gone after her husband with a carving knife. Because her actions were so serious, I decided to perform two SPECT studies on her. The first one was done four days before the onset of her period -- during the roughest time in her cycle -- and the second one was done eleven days later -- during the best time of her cycle.

My colleagues and I have observed that left-sided brain problems often correspond with a tendency toward significant irritability, even violence. Sherrie's premenstrual scan showed marked increased activity in her limbic system, particularly on the left side. Her post-menstrual scan, taken eleven days later, when Sherrie was her real self was normal! Contrary to the beliefs of some naysayers, PMS is a real thing. Women are not imagining things; the chemistry of their brain is genuinely altered and produces reactions they can neither understand nor control. For women like Sherrie (and their husbands), PMS can even be dangerous -- and must be paid attention to. I have seen the same general pattern in other couples I have counseled that I saw with Sherrie and her husband. During the best time of the woman's cycle, the two people like each other and get along. During the worst time there is fighting and alienation.

As I mentioned earlier, Depakote is often used for people who have cyclic mood disorders like manic-depressive disorder. Because Sherrie's SPECT findings showed an area of focal intensity in the left side of her limbic system (a finding I often see in someone who has a cyclic mood disorder), I put her on Depakote. It evened out her moods very nicely. Briefly, we tried taking her off it after nine months, but her symptoms returned to such a degree that her husband and best friend called me and begged me to put her back on it. Once again, two years seemed to be the magic number. It was only then that Sherrie was able to stop treatment without relapse.

People often ask me if men go through cycles. They do, but not in the same way as women. Men are prone to depression and moodiness because of everyday stresses. However, they are not subject to the more drastic hormonal changes that women are during certain periods: at the onset of puberty, during specific times in their menstrual cycles, in the period after they have had a baby, or during menopause. At these times women are far more vulnerable to limbic system problems than men are.

Some research suggests that women actually have a relatively larger limbic system than men do. This may account for the fact that women seem to be better at raising children -- they are more prone to connecting emotionally. The fact that men are less emotionally connected may explain their high suicide rate; men kill themselves three times more often than women. Since women are more in touch with their feelings, they are more likely to get help. Unfortunately, men suffer in isolation and then, out of hopelessness, feel there is no way out.

Chapter 3

IMAGES INTO ANXIETY
The Basal Ganglia

Functions

- integrates feeling and movement
- stores patterns of learned behavior
- stores programming from the past
- sets the body's idle or anxiety level

There's an area of the brain surrounding the limbic system called the basal ganglia. It contains some of the largest structures in the brain. The basalganglia is a processing center, and it controls a variety of functions critical to human behavior. It is involved with integrating feelings and move-ment; it stores patterns of learned behavior, stores programming from the past, and it is involved with the body's anxiety level.

The basal ganglia integrates feelings and movement. This is why you jump when you're excited, tremble when you're nervous or freeze when you are scared. W Mitchell, a well known motivational speaker, describes for audiences how he was involved in a fiery motorcycle accident on a street in San Francisco. As he lay burning on the ground, people stood nearby, frozen with fear, unable to move to help him. The intensity of emotion overwhelmed their basal ganglia. They were unable to move, even though most wanted to help.

Stored patterns of learned behavior are critical to human survival. Patterns such as how to be a mother, how to be a father, how to be a wife or husband are stored in this part of the brain. If you grew up watching a good mother or father, the patterns of behavior become stored in the basal ganglia and you have the tools to become a good mother or father. If you grew up watching a good role model for a husband or wife, those patterns become part of you, and the odds are in your favor that you'll have the tools to become a good husband or wife. If, on the other hand, you grew up watching ineffective parents, the odds are greater you will internalize those negative patterns of behavior and "automatically" go toward the coping mechanisms that became part of your experience.

Programming from the past is also chemically stored in this part of the brain. So, for example, if you were abused as a child, you store that as a pattern of behavior and your chances of abusing your own children increase. Your brain has been programmed that way. Or, for example, if you grew up in a family where your parents fought all of the time, you tend to pick somebody who fits with your programming and you fight all of the time.

As we go through life, our brain stores and categorizes many of the things we experience, especially those experiences that are charged with emotion. Each interaction that we witness or experience becomes chemically housed in the brain cells that are associated with that type of event. The information stored in these houses comes from many sources: such as significant childhood and teenage experiences at home, at school and with friends, along with significant adult experiences.

Once these patterns, thoughts and feelings are stored, they can be activated at moments' notice by an important association, unconsciously or without our awareness of what's happening. Our memory works through association, where one event triggers off memories of like events from the past. For example, if we saw our parents repeatedly handle conflict by yelling, screaming or even hitting each other, that pattern of behavior on fighting which is stored in the "marriage house" in the brain may be unconsciously turned on when as adults there is a fight or a disagreement.

Programmed behavior can significantly handicap your ability to stay in the present, in the moment. Here's an example: Rhonda grew up in a home where her parents continually fought with each other. The fights were major events. Nearly every week, her parents escalated the animosity to the point of yelling, screaming, throwing things, threats of divorce, and even hitting. Rhonda often hid in her room during the fights. She promised herself that she would be different. When she grew up her family, she vowed, would be calm and peaceful. Yet, when she got married, it was much like her family of origin. Whenever her husband disappointed her she would yell, scream, throw things, and threaten to leave him. She hated the scenes, but seemed unable to stop them. It was not until she was able to understand and connect the programming from the past that she was able to be more effective in her marriage.

Problems

- anxiety, nervousness
- panic attacks
- past patterns and programming control current behavior
- tendency to predict the worst
- abnormal movements with anxiety
- conflict avoidance

Clinically, we have seen that the basal ganglia also controls the body's idle, or the body's anxiety level. When it is overactive, there is a tendency to be anxious and nervous.

In my excitement over learning about SPECT, I studied the brain patterns of my own family, including my mother, my aunt, my wife, all three of my children and myself. I never felt more naked than when my own brain activity was projected onto a computer screen in front of my colleagues. I was happy to see that I had good brain activity in most of my brain. I saw an area, however, that looked like it was lit up like a red Christmas tree light bulb in the right side of my basal ganglia. It was working too hard. Of note, my mother (who tends to be a bit anxious) and my aunt (who clinically has been diagnosed with a panic disorder), all had the same pattern (increased activity in the right side of the basal ganglia). These blood flow patterns often run in families.

My whole life I have struggled with minor (or subclinical) issues of anxiety. Speaking in front of groups of people used to be very anxiety provoking for me. My first appearance on television was terrible. My hands sweated so much that I unknowingly rubbed my hands on my pants throughout the interview. Right before my second television interview, on the nationally syndicated Sonja Live program, I nearly had a panic attack while I was waiting to go on. I was flooded with negative thoughts and predicted disaster. I thought I would make a fool of myself, forget my own name, or stumble over my words. Recognizing what was happening, I started to chuckle to myself. I treated people who had this problem. I used the "Basal Ganglia Prescriptions" I give later in the book to successfully deal with the anxiety, and the interview went much better than the first one.

horizontal view
notice increase activity in right basal ganglia area (arrow)

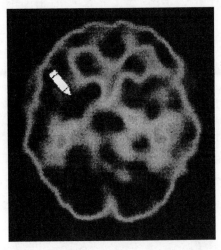

In addition to the issues of anxiety, I hate conflict. Any situation that triggers uncomfortable feelings, such as anxiety, causes a person to avoid the situation. Conflict avoidance has had a negative impact on parts of my life, leaving me unable to deal with some difficult situations at school or in business. As I thought about the increased activity in the right side of my basal ganglia, I understood that it was a pattern I inherited and it had a negative impact on my life, even though it never manifested itself in a clinical illness, like a panic disorder, which it had done in my aunt.

Panic Disorder

What are basal ganglia problems? Anxiety, nervousness, panic attacks. Almost all of the patients I have treated with a panic disorder whom I have scanned had abnormal activity in their basal ganglia. Here's an example of a patient with a panic disorder: Gary first came to see me about four years ago. He had first gone to his doctor and said, "I have back pain." The doctor examined

Gary's back and found a tender spot over his kidneys. He asked Gary to get a kidney X-ray.

In Gary's mind as soon as the doctor asked him to get this X-ray he thought, "The doctor is going to find out I have cancer." Notice the little leap in logic! But he didn't stop there. "The doctor's going to find out I have cancer. I'm going to have to have chemotherapy." So he's now in the treatment phase, 10 seconds into this. "I'm going to vomit my guts out, lose all my hair, be in a tremendous amount of pain, and then I'm going to die!" His mind did this all in a span of 30 seconds. Then Gary had a panic attack, where his heart beat fast, his hands got cold, and they started to sweat. He turned to the doctor and he said, "I can't have that X-ray." The doctor was bewildered! He said, "What do you mean? You came to see me to get help. You know you need this X- ray, so I can figure out..." Gary said, "No, you don't understand! I can't have the X-ray!" So the doctor found my number, called me and said, "Daniel, please help me with this guy." As Gary told me this story, I knew that he had a lifelong panic disorder. Gary was an expert at predicting the worst.

I taught Gary the "Basal Ganglia Prescriptions." I even went with him to have the X-ray because it was important to have it done quickly. I hypnotized him. He did wonderfully; he had great thoughts! He breathed in a relaxed way; he was doing very well and went through the procedure without any problems until the X-ray technician came into the room with a panicked look on his face, saying, "Gary, what side is your pain on?" Gary grabbed his chest, and then he looked at me like, "You SOB! I knew you were lying to me about this!" So I patted him on the leg and said, "Look Gary, before you die, let me take a look at the X-ray" (psychiatrists are also medical doctors). As I looked at his X-ray I could see that Gary had a big kidney stone, which was terribly painful, but kidney stones don't kill anybody! Gary's basal ganglia, which was working too hard, put him through tremendous pain by causing him to predict the worst possible outcome to situations. When there are basal ganglia problems, people have a tendency to predict the worst.

Marsha was a 36-year-old nurse when she first began experiencing panic attacks. Since her first episode, the panic attacks increased in frequency to the point where she stopped going out of her house, for fear that she'd have an attack and be unable to get help. She stopped working and made her husband take the children to and from school. Her symptoms included shortness of breath, heart palpitations, cold hands, a terrifying sense of impending doom, sweating and negative thinking. She was opposed to any medication, because in the past her mother, who also had panic attacks, was addicted to Valium. She did not want to see herself as being in any way like her mother. She believed that she "should" be able to control these attacks. Her husband, seeing her dysfunction only worsen, encouraged her to seek treatment.

Initially, she was in treatment with a family counselor. The counselor taught her relaxation and talking back to negative thoughts. It didn't help her. Her condition worsened and her husband brought her to see me. Given her resistance to medication I decided to order a SPECT study to evaluate her brain function.

Her SPECT study was abnormal. It revealed marked focal increased activity in the right side of her basal ganglia. This is a very common finding in patients who have a panic disorder. Interestingly, patients who have active seizure activity also have focal areas of increased activity in their brains. My colleagues and I wonder if the basal ganglia findings are the behavioral equivalent to seizures with the intense level of emotions associated with panic attacks.

horizontal view

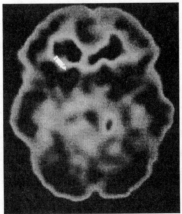

notice increase activity in right basal ganglia area (arrow)

The findings on her scan convinced Marsha to try medication. I put her on Xanax, an anti-anxiety medication. In a short period of time she became able to go out of her house, back to work and resume her life. In addition to the medication, I taught Marsha to become more assertive, taught her sophisticated biofeedback techniques and worked with her on correcting negative thoughts.

Several years later she was able to completely go off her medication and she remains "panic free."

A Case Of Post Traumatic Stress Disorder

Mark, a 50-year-old business executive, was admitted to the hospital shortly after he tried to kill himself. His wife had just started divorce proceedings against him, and he felt as though his life was falling apart. He was angry, hostile, frustrated, distrusting and chronically anxious. His co-workers felt that he was "mad all the time." He also complained of a constant headache. Mark was also a decorated Vietnam Veteran. He was an infantry soldier who had over 100 kills. He reported that he lost his humanity in Vietnam and that the experience made him "numb."

In the hospital, he said that he was tormented by the memories of the past. He felt that with his wife leaving him, he had no reason to live. Due to the severity of his symptoms, along with a history of a head injury in Vietnam, I ordered a brain SPECT study. It was abnormal. It showed marked increased activity in the left side of his basal ganglia. It was the most intense activity in that part of the brain that I had ever seen.

Left-sided basal ganglia findings are often seen in people who are chronically irritable or angry. Mood stabilizers, such as Lithium, Tegretol, or Depakote, are often helpful in decreasing the irritability. I placed Mark on Depakote. Almost immediately, his headaches went away and he began to feel calmer. The hospital staff noted how much calmer he was. He stopped snapping at everyone and he became more able to do the psychological work of healing from his divorce and healing the wounds from Vietnam.

In working with Mark I often felt that his experiences in Vietnam had reset his basal ganglia to be constantly on the alert. Nearly everyday for 13 months of the war, he had to be on alert in order to avoid being shot. Through the years, he never had the chance to learn how to reset his brain to a more normal level. The medication and therapy allowed him to relax and feel, for the first time in 25 years, that he had truly left the war zone.

Past Programming

Negative patterns from your past can control your present. I already discussed people who grew up in abusive environments. Their chances of abusing their own kids are very high unless they remember their childhood feelings and consciously decide to change the patterns from the past.

Let me give you an example from my life. When I was growing up, my father worked all the time. Literally, all the time! He owns a chain of grocery stores in Southern California, and the only time I would see him was when he took me to work. As I was growing up, I thought that working all the time was not such a good thing. I thought that dads should probably read to their kids, should go to their Little League games, and should spend time with their children's friends every now and again. But that's not what happened in my house! Even as a teenager, I told myself I would not be like my dad, as much as I loved him. I would spend a lot of time with my kids. Unconscious programming is much more powerful than desires. The unconscious message I got about being a man is that MEN WORK ALL THE TIME. So, if I don't think about it, what do you surmise I do? Work! All the time! It is programmed. I have had to develop reprogramming techniques to keep myself from working all the time and to help my patients overcome their own negative programming from the past. More on this in the "Basal Ganglia Prescriptions" chapter.

Conflict Avoidance

Anxiety is, by definition, very uncomfortable. Thus, people who are anxious tend to avoid any situations that make them uncomfortable, especially dealing with conflict. People who have basal ganglia problems run from conflict; they hate conflict. They don't want to deal with conflict. This conflict avoidance can have a serious negative impact on their lives.

I once treated a woman who used to work for a local oil company. Being very bright, she advanced very quickly in her career until she got to a certain position. At that level there were high-powered men who liked conflict, who liked confrontation, who were very competitive. She reacted by becoming quiet and subservient. She looked for ways to please these men to avoid the anxiety that she perceived would coincide with the conflict. Guess what happened? She stopped DEAD in her career. She was unable to confront others with her own ideas that may have been different from those of the others. The woman also had a severe panic disorder that prevented her from driving. Her husband and friends had to drive her everywhere because she was afraid she'd have a panic attack.

As she began treatment for her panic disorder and fear of driving, I taught her how to deal with the conflict. I taught her how to face these men and not run away from them. Subsequently, she began to speak up in meetings, stand up for her positions in the company and the upper management began to pay attention to her in a positive way.

It's very important to learn ways to soothe your basal ganglia. Otherwise, the anxiety and programming from the past will rule your life.

Chapter 4

IMAGES INTO EXPRESSION,
DISTRACTIBILITY AND IMPULSIVITY
The Prefrontal Cortex

Functions

- concentration
- attention span
- judgment
- impulse control
- organization
- critical thinking
- forward thinking
- ability to feel and express emotions

The prefrontal cortex is the most evolved part of the brain. It is at the front tip of the brain, underneath the forehead. It is the part of the brain that allows you to feel and express emotions; to feel happiness, sadness, joy, and love. It is different from the limbic system, which is a more primitive part of the brain. Even though the limbic system controls mood and libido, the prefrontal cortex is able to translate the feelings of the limbic system into recognizable feelings, emotions and words, such as love, passion or hate.

The prefrontal cortex also is involved with the day-to-day organizers of life, such as concentration, attention span, judgment, impulse control, planning and critical thinking. Our ability as a species to think, plan ahead and communicate with others is housed in this part of the brain.

When there are problems in the prefrontal cortex, the organization of daily life becomes difficult. People with prefrontal cortex problems often do things that they regret later, or have problems with impulsivity. They also experience problems with attention span, distractibility, procrastination, and poor judgment.

Test anxiety along with social anxiety also may be hallmarks of problems in the prefrontal cortex. Situations that require concentration, impulse control and quick reactions are often hampered by problems in the prefrontal cortex. Tests require concentration and the retrieval of information. Many people with prefrontal cortex problems experience difficulties in test situations because they have trouble activating this part of the brain, even if they have adequately prepared for the test. In a similar way, social situations require concentration, impulse control and dealing with uncertainty. Prefrontal cortex problems often cause people to "go blank" in these situations which lead to being uncomfortable in social situations.

When men have problems in this part of the brain, their emotions are often unavailable to them and their partners complain that they do not share their feelings. This can cause serious problems in a relationship because of how other people interpret the lack of expression of feeling. Many women, for example, blame their male partners for being cold or unfeeling, when it is really a problem in the prefrontal cortex that causes a lack of being "tuned in" to the feelings of the moment.

Prefrontal lobotomies, a surgical procedure severing fibers in the prefrontal cortex from the deeper structures in the brain, used in the late 1930s, 1940s, and 1950s to treat intractable or agitated psychotic patients often left the person listless, apathetic, distractible and expressionless. In the late 1950s, the procedure gave way to more effective psychotropic medications.

When scientists study the prefrontal cortex with neuroimaging studies like SPECT, it is often done twice. Once in a resting state, and again during a concentration task. In evaluating brain function, it is important to look at a working brain.

When the normal brain is challenged with a concentration task, such as math problems or sorting cards, the prefrontal cortex increases in activity. The more the brain is worked, the more energy is produced and increased blood flow occurs. In certain brain conditions, such as attention deficit disorder and schizophrenia, the prefrontal cortex decreases its activity in response to an intellectual challenge.

Problems

- short attention span
- distractibility
- impulse control problems
- social and test anxiety
- chronic lateness
- disorganization
- procrastination
- unavailability of emotions
- misperceptions
- poor judgement

Attention Deficit Disorder

Attention deficit disorder (ADD) is a neurobiological disorder characterized by a short attention span, distractibility, restlessness and impulsivity. ADD used to be thought of as a disorder of hyperactive boys who outgrew it before puberty. What we now know is that most people with ADD do not outgrow the symptoms of this disorder and that it frequently occurs in girls and women. It is estimated that ADD affects 17 million Americans. Other common symptoms of ADD clearly relate to functions of the prefrontal cortex, such as organizational problems, lack of ability to express emotions, problems with time, procrastination, and poor follow through on tasks.

Sally, age 40, was the very first person for whom I ordered a brain SPECT study. She was hospitalized for depression and anxiety in the psychiatric facility where I had privileges. In my clinical interview with her I discovered that she had problems with a short attention span, distractibility, restlessness and impulse control. In college, she never did term papers, she often spaced out in class, and many of her teachers told her that she was performing far below her potential. She dropped out of college after two years. In addition, she had a son who had

ADD. I ordered psychological testing to help me rule out the presence of a learning disability. I was surprised to learn that she had an IQ of 140. She had the potential to be anything she wanted, but was underemployed as a laboratory technician.

At the time Sally was in the hospital Alan Zametkin, MD from the National Institutes of Health had published a study in the New England Journal of Medicine on PET findings in ADD adults. PET studies are very similar to SPECT studies (nuclear medicine brain studies). Dr. Zametkin discovered that when ADD adults performed a concentration task there was decreased activity in the brain as opposed to increased activity that is what happened in the normal control group. This was a very exciting finding and correlated with some EEG research that I had previously done. It was shortly after I read Dr. Zametkin's paper that Dr. Jack Paldi (my nuclear medicine mentor) gave a lecture at my hospital on the use of brain SPECT studies in psychiatry. Given Sally's clinical presentation I decided to order a SPECT study on her. I called the University of Wisconsin, known for research in brain SPECT studies, and asked them how to perform the scans on ADD adults. They gave us their protocol, which was doing a resting study with the patient doing nothing, and then bringing her back two days later and having her perform a series of random math problems. Sally's studies were abnormal. At rest, she had good activity in her brain, especially in the prefrontal cortex. When she tried to concentrate, she had markedly decreased activity across her whole brain, especially in the prefrontal cortex! With that information I placed her on low dose Ritalin (a brain stimulant we use to treat ADD children). She had a wonderful response. Her mood was better, she was less anxious, and she could concentrate for longer periods of time. She eventually went back to school and finished her degree. No longer does she think of herself as an underachiever, but rather as someone who needs treatment for a medical problem. She says, "Having ADD is like needing glasses. When someone needs glasses it is not because they are dumb, crazy, or stupid. It is just that their eyes are shaped funny. The glasses help them see properly. With ADD, I'm not dumb, crazy, or stupid, I just need the medication to help me feel calm and to be able to concentrate." The scan and her response to medication changed the whole perception she had about herself.

 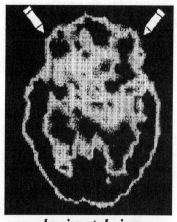

horizontal view
at rest
full frontal activity

horizontal view
during a concentration task
marked decreased frontal activity

Brian was 24 years old when he first came to see me. He came for help because he had gone to a junior college six straight semesters. He wasn't able to finish one of them! He wanted to go to medical school. Everybody told him he was nuts! How could he go to medical school if he couldn't even finish a junior college semester? Then his mother read a flyer on my book, <u>Windows Into The ADD Mind</u>. She wondered if Brian didn't have attention deficit disorder.

After I took Brian's history, it was clear he had suffered from an undiagnosed case of ADD his whole life. From the time he was in kindergarten, he had problems staying in his seat, he was restless, distractible, disorganized and labeled as an underachiever.

Brian's father wanted to be convinced about ADD and requested we do a brain SPECT study to look at his brain. He wanted to make sure Brian wasn't just looking for another excuse as to why he was failing in life. His brain SPECT study at rest was normal. When Brian tried to concentrate, however, the prefrontal cortex of his brain turned off.

After the results of the clinical examination and brain SPECT studies, I put Brian on Ritalin, a stimulant medication that has been used to treat symptoms of ADD for over 40 years. Brian had a remarkable response. He completed all of his classes at school the next semester. In 18 months he got his Associates of Arts Degree and three years later he finished his Bachelor's Degree in biology. He has been accepted to medical school! It's amazing how much his father's attitude has changed towards him.

He told me, "I thought he was just lazy. It makes me sad to think of all those years that he had a medical problem and I justhassled him for being lazy. I wish I could have those years back."

I understood how Brian's father felt. I adopted my oldest son, Antony, when he was two-and-a-half-years-old. He was an intelligent child who was tested as gifted in the second grade. By fourth grade, he complained of being bored in school. A half an hour of homework would take him three or four hours to do. He was often distracted, restless and off task. He began to slip a little in school in seventh grade, and by ninth grade he fell apart and did terrible in school. I took him to see a colleague of mine who evaluated him. He said that my son was very bright, but that he had trouble concentrating and was easily distracted. He felt that my son might have ADD. Yet, Antony was never really a hyperactive child. In fact, if anything he was spacy, daydreamy, and a little sluggish. Approximately half the children, teens and adults who have ADD are not hyperactive; in fact they may be hypoactive. I decided to do a SPECT study on Antony. I had tears in my eyes as I looked at his SPECT study. Like Brian, he had good activity in his prefrontal cortex at rest, but when he tried to concentrate his prefrontal cortex completely turned off. For years I had been telling him to try harder. Boy, did I feel like a fool. Medication has helped Antony a lot. He's now in college and making a remarkable turnaround from where he had been 4 years earlier.

Epidemiologists estimate that about three to five percent of the population has attention deficit disorder. In children, this pattern of frontal lobe turnoff often correlates with hyperactivity. Those kids are INTO EVERYTHING!! They have a short attention span, are distractible, seek conflict, seek stimulation; they have a very real problem! However, we know that these kids don't just outgrow it! As adults, they have problems with short attention spans, impulsivity, chronic lateness, disorganization, and poor handwriting.

I have one man in my practice that has 10 businesses, because that's what he needed in order to keep himself turned on! When the brain is underactive, it's uncomfortable! Unconsciously, people learn how to turn it on, either by coffee, cigarettes (both mild stimulants), anger, a fast paced life, or doing highly stimulating activities, such as Bungee jumping. Bungee jumpers need to be screened for this problem.

Many psychiatric disorders are now thought to have significant genetic influences. ADD is no exception. Here's a family case example:

Paul, age 20, first came to see me because he was having trouble finishing his senior year at a Northern California university. He was having trouble completing term papers, he could not focus in class and he had little motivation. He began to believe that he should drop out of school and go to work for his father. He hated the idea of quitting school so close to graduation. He came to see me on a referral from a friend who had a younger brother whom I had helped. In his history, Paul also told me about bouts of depression that had been treated with Prozac in the past with little benefit. Paul's brain SPECT study was consistent with both depression and ADD. The SPECT study showed increased activity in his limbic system (consistent with depression) and deactivation of his prefrontal cortex during a concentration task (consistent with ADD). He had a wonderful response to a combination of an antidepressant and stimulant medication. He finished college and got the kind of job he wanted.

When Paul's mother, Pam, saw what a nice response he had to treatment, she came to see me for herself. As a child, she had trouble learning. Even though she was very artistic, she had little motivation for school and her teachers labeled her as an underachiever. As an adult, Pam went back to school and earned her degree in elementary school teaching. In order to student teach, however, she had to pass the National Teacher's Exam. She had failed the test on four occasions. Pam was ready to give up and try a new avenue of study when she saw Paul get better. She thought maybe there was help for her. In fact, her brain SPECT studies were very similar to Paul's studies and she responded to the same combination of medication. Four months later, she passed the National Teacher's Exam.

With two successes in the family, the mother then sent her 19-year-old daughter, Karen, to see me. Like her brother, Karen was a bright child who had underachieved in school. At the time she came to see, me she lived in Los Angeles and she was enrolled in a broadcast journalism course. She complained that learning the material was hard for her. She was also moody, restless, easily distracted, impulsive and had a quick temper. Several years earlier she was treated for alcohol abuse and using amphetamines. She said that the alcohol settled her restlessness and the amphetamines helped her to concentrate. Karen's brain SPECT studies were very similar to her brother's and mother's. Once on medication, she was amazed at the difference. She could concentrate in class and she finished her work in half the time as before. Karen's level of confidence increased to the point where she could go and look for work as a broadcaster, something she had been unable to do previously.

The most reluctant member of the family to see me was the father, Tim. Even though Pam, Paul and Karen told him that he should see me, he balked at the idea. He said, "There's nothing wrong with me; look at how successful I am." But his family knew different. Even though Tim owned a successful grocery store, he was reclusive and distant. He got tired early in the day, he was easily distracted and he was scattered in his approach to work. He was successful at work, in part, because he had very good people who took his ideas and made them happen. He also had trouble learning new games, such as cards. This caused him to avoid many social situations. Tim enjoyed high stimulation activities and he loved riding motorcycles, even at the age of 55. Looking back, Tim had done poorly in high school. He barely passed college even though he had a very high IQ. He tended to drift from job to job until he was able to buy the grocery store from a widow whose husband had recently died. Tim's wife finally convinced him to see me. She was getting ready to divorce him, because he would never talk with her in the evening. She felt that he didn't care about her. He later told me that he was physically and emotionally drained.

During my first session with Tim he told me that he couldn't possibly have ADD because he was a success in business. But the more questions I asked him about his past, the more lights went on in his head. His nickname was "Speedy" as a child. He often didn't do his homework. He was often distracted or bored in school. His energy was gone by the end of the morning. When I asked about his organization at work, he replied her name was Elsa, his assistant. At the end of the interview, my comment back to him was that, "If you really do have ADD, I wonder how successful you could be given what you've already accomplished." Tim's brain SPECT studies showed the classic pattern for ADD. When he tried to concentrate the prefrontal cortex of his brain turned off, rather than on. When I told him this, it really sunk in. "Maybe that is why it is hard for me to learn games. When I'm in a social situation and I'm pressed to learn or respond, I just freeze up. So I avoid these situations."

Tim had a remarkable response to Ritalin. He was more awake during the day, he accomplished more in less time and his relationship with his wife dramatically improved. In fact, they both said they couldn't believe that their relationship could be so good, after all the years of distance and hurt.

Psychotic Disorders

Psychotic disorders, such as schizophrenia, are serious disorders that affect a person's ability to distinguish reality from fantasy. These disorders are complex, but at least in part, they affect the function of the prefrontal cortex.

Schizophrenia is a chronic, long-standing disorder characterized by "psychotic symptoms" that significantly impair functioning and involve disturbances in feeling, thinking, and behavior. Delusions, hallucinations, and distorted thinking characterize this disorder. When I first started ordering SPECT studies on Schizophrenic patients, I began to understand why they distorted incoming information. Julie is a good example:

Julie was 48 years old when we met. She was divorced and she had a history of multiple hospitalizations for paranoid thinking, hearing voices, feeling electrical blasting in her head, along with delusional thinking. Her main delusion centered around being assaulted by someone who put an electrical probe inside of her head which "blasts her with electricity." She had been on multiple medication trials without success. Due to her lack of responsiveness to standard treatments I ordered a brain SPECT study.

In a sense, Judith was right. She was being blasted with electricity (note the multiple hot spots across her brain), but because she had such poor prefrontal cortex activity she was unable to process the physiological nature of her illness and developed delusions in order to explain the pain she experienced. With the information from the SPECT study, Judith was placed on a high therapeutic dose of Depakote that lessened her pain and anxiety. For the first time, she was willing to entertain the possibility that symptoms were the result of abnormal brain activity rather than from an outside attacker. A repeat SPECT study 8 months later showed a marked decrease in the hot spots in her brain along with subsequent increased activity in her prefrontal cortex.

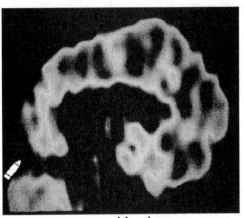

side view
schizophrenia
marked decreased prefrontal activity
and multiple hot spots across the cortex

In another case, Derrick, a 13-year-old boy came to see me because he was severely anxious. He was displaying psychotic symptoms, feeling that other children were talking about him behind his back and that they were out to embarrass him in front of the whole school. He started to avoid all contact with his peer group. He would hide in the middle of clothes racks at the mall if he saw people he knew, for fear that they might start to laugh at him or talk about him to others. He was petrified by his thoughts and he stopped going to school. He even seriously entertained suicide as a way to rid himself of the awful thoughts. He had crying spells, sleeplessness and intense anxiety. No one was able to rationally discuss these feelings with him and he was unable to entertain other alternatives for his thoughts. I saw him for months in psychotherapy and tried him on several antidepressant and antipsychotic medications without a therapeutic response. His psychological testing, especially the inkblottest, revealed psychotic thinking. A SPECT scan was done when he was off all medication to help us understand what was going on.

Derrick's SPECT study showed marked decreased activity in his prefrontal cortex at rest, which is a common finding in psychotic disorders. It is also a finding in some psychotic depressions. The study led me to try alternative medications that were more effective. Within two months there was a dramatic clinical improvement in his condition. His mood was better, there were no suicidal thoughts, he was less sensitive to others and he was more able to entertain alternatives to his distorted thoughts. Seven months later, he was much more like a normal teenager. A repeated SPECT study was performed 6 months later with normalization of prefrontal cortex activity. Four years later, I see Derrick every couple of months. He is a senior in high school and on the student council.

The SPECT study was very important in the treatment process. It clearly showed Derrick's parents that his problems were based on brain abnormalities and that he couldn't help what he thought or felt. They were able to react in a more understanding and helpful manner, changing the level of stress at home.

As the prefrontal cortex is the most evolved part of the brain, optimizing its function will significantly enhance your chances for success in whatever you do.

Chapter 5

IMAGES INTO OBSESSIONS
The Cingulate System

Functions

- allows shifting of attention
- cognitive flexibility
- helps the mind move from idea to idea
- gives the ability to see options
- helps you go with the flow

At the top, in the middle of the frontal lobes is an area of the brain termed the "cingulate gyrus." It's the part of the brain that allows you to shift your attention from thing to thing, to move from idea to idea, to see the options in life. Feelings of safety and security have also been attributed to this part of the brain. In my experience, the term that best relates to this part of the brain is cognitive flexibility.

Cognitive flexibility deals with a person's ability to go with the flow, adapt to changes, successfully deal with new situations. There are many situations in life where cognitive flexibility is essential. For example, starting a new job requires people to learn a new system of doing things. Even if you did something another way at a previous employment, learning how to shift to please a new boss or adapt to a new system is critical to job success. Junior high school students need cognitive flexibility in order to be successful in school. In 7th grade, many students begin having multiple teachers throughout the day. It is necessary to shift learning styles in order to adapt to the different styles posed by the teachers. Flexibility is also important in friendships. What works in a friendship with one person may not at all be effective with someone else.

Effectively managing change and transitions is an essential ingredient for both personal, interpersonal and business growth. The cingulate system of the brain can be of great help or hindrance to this process. When it is working properly we are more able to roll with the circumstances of the day. When it is impaired or "overactive" cognitive flexibility is diminished.

The cingulate system has also been implicated in "future oriented thinking," such as planning and goal setting. When this part of the brain works well it is easier to plan and set reasonable goals. On the negative side, difficulties in this part of the brain can cause a person to predict negative events and feel very unsafe in the world.

Problems

- worrying
- cognitive inflexibility
- holds onto hurts from the past
- stuck on thoughts (obsessions)
- stuck on behaviors (compulsions)
- oppositional behavior
- argumentativeness
- addictive behaviors (alcohol abuse, eating disorders, chronic pain)

When the cingulate system is abnormal, as it was in the story of Willie in Chapter One, people have a tendency to get stuck on things, to get the same thought in their heads over and over and over! They may become worriers and continually obsess on the same thought. The may hold onto hurts or grudges from the past, being unable to let them go. They may also get stuck on negative behaviors, or develop compulsions such as hand washing or excessively checking locks.

One patient who had difficulties in this part of the brain described this phenomenon to me saying it was "like being on a rat's exercise wheel, where the thoughts just go over and over and over." Another patient told me, "It's like having a reset button that is always on. Even though I don't want to have the thought anymore, it just keeps coming back."

The clinical problems associated with the cingulate will be discussed shortly. There are also a number of what I call "subclinical patterns" associated with abnormalities in this part of the brain. The term "subclinical" relates to problems that many people have which do not reach the intensity or cause the dysfunction of a disorder. Examples of these as they relate to the cingulate gyrus include worrying, holding onto hurts from the past, developing a "first impression" of someone and not changing your mind as incoming information changes, and being rigid.

Worrying

Overactivity in the cingulate is often associated with worrying, or getting locked into negative thoughts that you think about over and over. Something upsets you and you can't let go of it, or you have a "future concern" which recycles through your brain. Even though we all worry at times (and some worry is necessary to keep us working or studying in school), people who have an overactive cingulate may have worrying as part of their personality. They may worry to the point of causing emotional and physical harm to themselves. Whenever you have repetitive negative concerns that circle through your mind it can cause tension, stress, stomach aches, headaches and irritability. Chronically expressing worries often irritates others and makes a person look less powerful and perhaps even less mature.

At a dinner party, an old friend of mine (who is also a physician) complained that his wife worried "all the time." "She worries for the whole family," he told me. It upsets the children and me. Her constant worry seemed to be associated with her chronic headaches and irritability. "How do I help her relax so that she won't get so upset about the little things in life," he queried. I had known my friend's wife for more than 15 years. Even though she had never been clinically depressed and wouldn't fit the diagnostic criteria for panic disorder or OCD (obsessive-compulsive disorder) I knew that it was in her personality to worry. Members in her family, which she had discussed with me on several occasions, did have clinical problems (such as alcoholism, drug abuse and compulsive behaviors) associated with the cingulate system.

Holding On To Hurts

Holding on tightly to hurts from the past can cause serious problems in a person's life. Again, the underlying brain mechanism for this problem is often a person's inability to shift away from a pattern of thought, due to an overactive cingulate. Something negative happened in the past and the person cannot let go of it. For example, I once treated a woman who was very angry with her husband. On trip to Hawaii her husband allowed his eyes to wander onto some of the scantily dressed women on the beach at Waikiki. When she saw his eyes wander and pause she became irate. She felt he had been unfaithful to her with his eyes. Her anger ruined the whole trip and she continued to bring up the incident years later.

Cognitive Inflexibility

Cognitive inflexibility is the root of most cingulate problems. It is the need to have things just a certain way or you become very upset. It is hard to "go with the flow" or roll with the ups and downs of everyday life. While I was working on this chapter during a visit at a friend's house his six-year-old daughter, Kimmy gave me a perfect example of cognitive inflexibility. Her older sister was instructed by my friend to get Kimmy ready to go out for the day. She picked out a shirt and pair of pants for her sister. Kimmy complained that the shirt and pants looked stupid. She had the same complaint for the next three outfits that her sister chose for her. Kimmy wanted to wear a sundress (it was February and cold outside). She cried and cried to get her way. Nothing else would do. Once she got the idea of the sun dress in her head she couldn't shift away from it.

In couples counseling through the years I have frequently heard another example of cognitive inflexibility: the need to do something NOW. Not five minutes from now, but now! Here's a fairly common scenario. A wife asks her husband to get some clothes out of the dryer and put the clothes from the washer into the dryer. He asks her to wait a few minutes because he's watching the end of a basketball game. She becomes irate and says that it needs to be done NOW. They get into a fight. She doesn't feel comfortable until the chore is finished. He feels intruded upon, pushed around, and generally degraded. The need to DO IT NOW can cause some serious relational problems.

There are many more everyday examples of trouble shifting attention or cognitive inflexibility. Here's a short list:

- only eating specific foods, being unwilling to try new tastes
- having to keep a room a certain way
- having to make love the same way every time (or avoiding lovemaking because of feeling uncomfortable about the messiness that is involved with it)
- becoming upset if the plans for the evening change at the last minute
- having to do things a certain way at work, even if it's not in the business' best interest (i.e., not being flexible to meet an important customer's needs)
- having other family members do chores in a certain way, such as the dishes, or you become upset (this often alienates others and they become less willing to help

Cognitive inflexibility insidiously can destroy happiness, joy and intimacy.

Obsessive-Compulsive Disorder

On the outside, Gail was normal. She went to work every day, she was married to her high school sweetheart, and she had two small children. On the inside, Gail felt like a mess. Her husband was ready to leave her and her children were often withdrawn and upset. Gail was distant from her family and locked into the private hell of obsessive-compulsive disorder. She cleaned her house for hours every night after work. She screamed at her husband and children when anything was out of place. She would become especially hysterical if she saw a piece of hair on the floor, and she was often at the sink washing her hands. She also made her husband and children wash their hands more than ten times a day. She stopped making love to her husband because she couldn't stand the feeling of being messy.

On the verge of divorce, Gail and her husband came to see me. At first, her husband was very skeptical about the biological nature of her illness. Gail's brain SPECT study showed marked increased activity in the cingulate system, demonstrating that she really did have trouble shifting her attention.

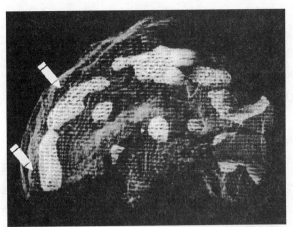

3-D side view looking at the most active areas
marked increased activity in the cingulate gyrus

With this information, I placed Gail on Zoloft. Within six weeks, she had significantly relaxed, her ritualistic behavior had diminished and she stopped making her kids wash their hands every time they turned around. Her husband couldn't believe the change. Gail was more like the woman he married.

Obsessive-compulsive disorder (OCD) affects somewhere between two to four million people in the US. This disorder, almost without exception, dramatically impairs a person's functioning and often affects the whole family. OCD is often a secretive disorder to the outside world, but not to those who live with the person.

The hallmarks of this disorder are obsessions (recurrent disgusting or frightening thoughts) or compulsions (behaviors that a person knows make no sense but feels compelled to do anyway). The obsessive thoughts are usually senseless, repugnant and invade consciousness. They may involve repetitive thoughts of violence (such as killing one's child), contamination (such as becoming infected by shaking hands) or doubt (such as having hurt someone in a traffic accident, even though no such accident occurred). Many efforts are made to suppress or resist these thoughts, but the more a person tries to control them, the more powerful they become.

The most common compulsions involve hand-washing, counting, checking and touching. These behaviors are often performed according to certain rules in a very strict or rigid manner. For example, a person with a counting compulsion may feel the need to count every crack on the pavement on their way to work or school. What would be a five-minute walk for most people could turn into a three or four hour trip for the person with obsessive-compulsive disorder. They have an urgent insistent sense of "I have to do it" inside. A part of the individual generally recognizes the senselessness of the behavior and doesn't get pleasure from carrying it out, although doing it often provides a release of tension.

The intensity of OCD varies widely. Some people have mild versions, where, for example, they have to have the house perfect before they go on vacation or they spend the vacation, worrying about the condition of the house. The more serious forms can cause a person to be house bound for years. I once treated an 83-year-old woman, who had obsessive, sexual thoughts that made her feel dirty inside. It got to the point where she would lock all her doors, draw all the window shades, turn off the lights, take the phone off the hook and sit in the middle of a dark room trying to catch the abhorrent sexual thoughts as they came into her mind. It got to the point where her life became paralyzed by this behavior and she needed to be hospitalized.

Exciting research in the past few years has shown a biological pattern associated with OCD. Brain SPECT studies have shown increased blood flow in the cingulate system, along with increased activity in the basal ganglia (often the anxiety component of the problem). Again, this part of the brain is responsible for allowing a person to shift his or her attention from subject to subject. When this area is overactive, a person gets "stuck" on the same thought or behavior.

Like most forms of mental illness, OCD has a biological basis and part of effective treatment usually involves medication. At this writing there are eight "anti-obsessive medications" and there are more on the way. Before 1987 there were no good medications to treat OCD. The current medications that have shown promise with OCD are Anafranil (clomipramine), Prozac (fluoxetine), Zoloft (sertraline), Paxil (paroxetine), Effexor (venlafaxine), Remeron (mirtazapine) and Serzone (nefazodone) and Luvox (fluvoxamine). These medications have provided many patients with profound relief from OCD symptoms. In addition, behavior therapy is often helpful for these patients. This is where a patient is gradually exposed to the situations most likely to bring out the rituals and habits. Behavior techniques also include thought stopping-techniques and strong urging by the therapist for the patient to face his or her worst fear (for example, having a patient with a dirt or contamination fear play in the mud).

OCD Spectrum Disorders

There is a group of disorders that have been recently labeledas obsessive-compulsive spectrum disorders. It is based on the premise that these disorders occur because the person experiences repetitive unwanted thoughts or behaviors. They tend to get stuck on thoughts and cannot get them out of their minds unless they act in a specific manner. According to psychiatrist Ronald Pies, M.D., postulated OCD spectrum disorders have included: trichotillomania (pulling out one's own hair), onychophagia (nail biting), Gilles de la Tourette's Syndrome (involuntary motor and vocal tics), kleptomania, body dysmorphic disorder (feeling a part of the body is excessively ugly), hypochondria, autism, compulsive shopping, pathological gambling, chronic pain, addictive disorders and eating disorders.

A sample of repetitive thoughts that significantly interfere with behavior might include:

-- chronic pain, "I hurt! I hurt! I hurt!"

-- eating disorders, such as anorexia and bulimia, "I'm too fat! I'm too fat! I'm too fat!", despite rational evidence to the contrary.

-- addictive disorders, "I need a drink! I need a drink!"

-- pathological gambling, "Next time I'll win! Next time I'll win! Next time I'll win!"

-- compulsive shopping, "I need to buy this one thing! I need to buy this one thing! I need to buy this one thing,"

-- oppositional defiant disorder, "No I won't! You can't make me!

In 1991, Susan Swedo, M.D. at the National Institutes of Mental Health in Bethesda, Maryland hypothesized that patients with trichotillomania would exhibit the same brain imaging as those with OCD. However, at rest these patients exhibited a different brain pattern. Yet, when these patients were treated with the anti-obsessive antidepressant Anafranil there was decreased activity in the top, middle aspects of the frontal lobes, which has also been found with successful treatment of OCD with anti-obsessive antidepressants.

Here are several case examples from my own practice to illustrate OCD spectrum disorders:

Chronic Pain

Stewart, a 40-year-old roofer, hurt his back ten years ago when he fell off a roof. He underwent six back operations but remained in constant pain. He was essentially bedridden and about to lose his family because all he could think about was the pain. The threat of losing his family catalyzed him to get a psychiatric evaluation. His SPECT revealed marked overactivity in the cingulate system. He was placed on Anafranil 200 mg. a day. After 5 weeks, he reported that his back still hurt, but he was much less focused on the pain. He was able to get out of bed and start back to school. Other researchers have also reported several cases of intractable pain that were also responsive to treatment with anti-obsessive medications.

Eating Disorders

Twenty-year-old Leslie suffered from bulimia for three years. She got to the point where she was using laxatives several times a day in increasing doses, along with exercising for two to three hours a day. Her binges were also becoming more frequent. When she sought treatment, she felt totally out of control. During her initial evaluation, she said she knew her behavior was abnormal and she hated it. However, when she got the urge to eat, she felt she had to give in to it and afterwards she could not get the thoughts of being overweight out of her head. She had a maternal aunt who had been diagnosed with obsessive-compulsive disorder. Her brain SPECT study revealed increased activity in the cingulate system along with increased activity in her right basal ganglia. With this information, she was placed in an eating disorders group and given Prozac (an anti-obsessive antidepressant) up to 80 mg. Over the next three months, she improved markedly to the point where she was eating normally, not taking any laxatives at all, and exercising less than an hour a day.

In 1992, the Prozac Bulimia Nervosa Collaborative Study Group (1992) reported that therapy with 60 mg. of Prozac significantly decreased the frequency of binge-eating and self-induced vomiting. Prozac has been reported in the medical literature to decrease activity in the top, middle portions of the frontal lobes in obsessive-compulsive patients.

Drug or Alcohol Addictions

Joshua began using drugs and alcohol at the age of twelve. When his parents finally caught on to his drug abuse at the age of sixteen, Joshua reported he had used LSD more than a hundred times and that he was drinking a pint of whiskey a day. He said that he was unable to stop, even though he wanted to many times. When his parents brought him in for evaluation, it was revealed that he had a strong history of drug and alcohol abuse on both sides of his family, even though neither of his parents drank alcohol or abused drugs. After his SPECT study revealed significant overactivity in the cingulate system, Joshua was placed on Zoloft in addition to his individual and support group therapy. He reported that he still had periodic cravings for the substances, but that he could break them more easily with the behavioral techniques he learned. He was able to get the thoughts about drugs and alcohol out of his head.

Pathological Gambling

Many people enjoy gambling. They feel happy when they win. Discouraged when they lose. And they realize that gambling is a game of chance, like many things in life. Some people, however, become addicted to gambling and it can ruin every aspect of their lives. Pathological gambling, defined by the American Psychiatric Association, is persistent and recurrent maladaptive gambling behavior that disrupts personal, family or vocational pursuits. Pathological gambling usually starts with an important "big win." The high from the win gets "stuck" in a gambler's head and they begin to chase it, even to the point of their own destruction.

Adam came to our office out of desperation. His wife had just left him and he had seen an attorney to discuss filing bankruptcy. His gambling had gotten out of control. He was a successful entrepreneur who had worked hard at starting his own business, but in the few years before he came to see me, he began neglecting his business spending more of his time at the race track and driving back and forth to Reno and Lake Tahoe in Nevada. In our first session he told me, "I feel compelled to gamble. I know it is ruining my life, but it seems I have to place a bet or the tension just builds and builds. Before I started losing everything I knew I could win. It was all I thought about!" Adam had come from an alcoholic home. Both his father and paternal grandfather were alcoholics. Even though Adam never had a problem with alcohol he clearly had an addiction. Explaining the cingulate system to Adam was helpful. He could identify many people in his family who had problems shifting attention. "You should see our family gatherings," he told me, "someone is always mad at someone else. People in my family can hold grudges for years and years." In addition to going to Gamblers Anonymous and being seen in psychotherapy I prescribed a small dose of Prozac for him to help him shift away from the obsessive thoughts about gambling. Eventually, he was able to reconnect with his wife and rebuild his business.

Compulsive Spending

Compulsive shopping is another manifestation of problems in the cingulate system. Compulsive shoppers get high from the pursuit and purchase of goods. They act compulsively (or as if they cannot help what they are doing, even though they promise themselves they won't spend) and spend inordinate amounts of time thinking about shopping activities. This addiction can ruin a person's financial status, along with their marriage and have a negative impact on their work.

Jill worked as the office manager for a big law firm in San Francisco. Before work, during her lunch hours and after work she found herself drawn to the stores at Union Square, near her office. She felt compelled to shop. She had a rush of internal excitement as she picked out clothes for herself and other family members. She also enjoyed buying presents for others, even if they were just acquaintances. It was the act of shopping that was important. Even though she knew she should not be spending the money she felt out of control. It felt too good to stop. She and her husband had many fights over the money she spent during her shopping sprees. She also began embezzling money from work. She took care of the checkbook and began a pattern of writing extra checks to a fictitious vendor in order to cover her debt. When a business audit almost found her out she stopped. But her addiction didn't. Divorce between her and her husband finally came when he uncovered a credit card debt in the amount of $30,000. Ashamed, scared and depressed Jill entered treatment. All her life she had been a worrier. In her teens she had had an eating disorder and she had a cousin who had an obsessive-compulsive disorder. Her SPECT study revealed a markedly overactive cingulate system. When she got locked into a train of thought or behavior (spending) she had real problems shifting away from it. Zoloft (an anti-obsessive antidepressant) was helpful for her as part of the healing process.

Oppositional Defiant Disorder

Contumacious: stubborn resistance to authority (get stuck on saying No).

One of the most interesting findings among the patients we studied was that mothers who had obsessive thoughts or compulsive behaviors tended to have children with oppositional defiant disorder. There were five cases when this parent-child pattern occurred where we obtained brain SPECT studies on both the mother and the child. In these cases both the mother and the child's brain SPECT study revealed increased activity in the top, middle portions of their frontal lobes. Both a biological explanation for the clinical finding along with a psychological or behavioral etiology need be entertained. One can postulate that the finding of increased activity in the top, middle part of the frontal lobes (biological component) can cause the mothers to have problems shifting attention and become stuck on anxiety-provoking thoughts, while the child's inability to shift attention causes his behavior to appear oppositional. It is also possible that the mother's overprotectiveness (the behavioral part) induces the oppositional behavior and the subsequent SPECT finding.

As mentioned above, it has been observed that the brain SPECT abnormalities in the top, middle portions of the frontal lobes normalize with effective treatment. This does not appear to be inter-test variability, as researchers have shown that without intervening in some way the brain SPECT patterns vary little from test to test. The following is a case of oppositional defiant disorder where follow-up data was obtained.

Jason, age 9, was evaluated for significant oppositional behavior. He was suspended from school five times in second grade for refusing to do what he was told and being openly defiant with his teacher. His parents were told not to bring him back to school until they sought professional help. His clinical evaluation was also consistent with a diagnosis of oppositional defiant disorder. His brain SPECT study revealed marked increased activity in the top, middle portions of his frontal lobes. When he improved only minimally with behavioral interventions he was placed on Anafranil. Within two weeks, he showed marked clinical improvement. After two months, his brain SPECT study was repeated and revealed essentially normal activity in the medial portions of his frontal lobes. The following year, Jason was not suspended from school and his teacher that year could not understand why the other teachers had warned her about him.

Stress Often Increases Activity in the Cingulate System

In many children and teenagers with oppositional defiant disorder, I obtained both a rest and concentration SPECT study. I wanted to see what happened to the cingulate system when they tried to concentrate. Interestingly, in about half of the cases, I saw a further increase in activity in the top, middle portion of the frontal lobes during the concentration task. Clinically, I find that this correlates with those oppositional children and teens who get worse ("more stuck") under pressure or when they are pushed to comply with certain requests. I have seen this occur frequently on an adolescent treatment unit. One of these teens would become so "stuck" that they would refuse to comply with the staff requests and end up on restriction or even, in some cases, in restraints because they could not shift their attention to more effective behavior.

One evening, I had a dramatic example of this in my own family. My wife and two daughters came to my office to pick me up and go out to dinner. My youngest daughter smiled when she saw me and gave me a big hug. As we were going to drive in two separate cars I said to her, "Come on, Kaitlyn, ride with me in my car." Kaitlyn has been diagnosed with attention deficit disorder and she is often a handful. I wanted to spend some extra time with her on the way to the restaurant. As soon as I said, "Come with me," she said, "No. I don't want to." My feelings were a little hurt. I replied, "Come on, Kaitlyn, I want to be with you." She said, "NO! I'm going with mommy." As I am not one to give up easily,

I picked her up and put her in the car. She yelled, screamed, and cried half way to the restaurant (real quality time). I was feeling lousy when all of a sudden she stopped crying, dried her eyes, and said, "I'm sorry, daddy. I really wanted to go with you." When I pushed Kaitlyn to go with me, her brain locked. She became unable to think about what she wanted to do and she got stuck on her first reaction.

Kaitlyn's SPECT study showed increased activity in the top, middle portion of her frontal lobes. All of my children are grandchildren of alcoholics. I have seen a significant connection between a family history of alcoholism and increased activity in the cingulate system.

Given that children and teens with oppositional defiant disorder tend to get cognitively "locked up" when they are pushed to comply, I have found using behavioral techniques such as giving options and distraction more effective in obtaining compliance. When you give an oppositional child or teen an option as to when they might do something they tend to be less likely to get stuck on "No, I won't do it." When they are stuck on a negative thought or behavior, I have found it helpful to distract them for a bit and then come back to the issue at hand later. I would have been better at getting Kaitlyn to go with me in the car if I had given her a choice to go rather than just telling her she was going to go.

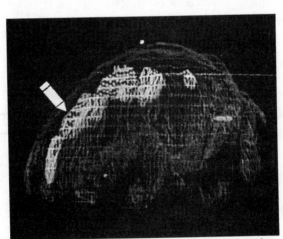

3-D side view looking at the most active areas
marked increased activity in the cingulate gyrus

Therapy of a Family with Like Brain SPECT Findings

The following family case studies demonstrate how the same brain finding can present itself clinically in different ways. Brain SPECT studies were obtained on a mother and two of her children. The studies proved to be useful in understanding the family dynamics and in the diagnosis and treatment of this family system.

Celina is a 36-year-old Hispanic female who experienced depressive feelings after the birth of her first child ten years prior to her evaluation. She experienced significant irritability, crying spells, sleeplessness, lack of appetite and weight loss, problems concentrating and being unable to manage her children. Her condition was brought to a crisis with suicidal behavior when she separated from her husband. She was initially seen by another psychiatrist and started on an antidepressant, which had little effect. I started to see her in psychotherapy and placed her on a different antidepressant. It had a positive effect and she did well in psychotherapy. After several months, she decided that she "should be stronger than the depression" and took herself off the medication. Within several weeks her depression worsened, but she was resistant to restarting her antidepressant.

In an effort to demonstrate to her that her depression existed on a biological level as well as on a psychological level, a brain SPECT study was performed. Celina's SPECT brain study revealed increased activity in her limbic system (consistent with the underlying depressive disorder) and marked increased activity in the top, middle portions of her frontal lobes.

With the increased activity in the top, middle portions of her frontal lobes, I asked her more pointed obsessive-compulsive disorder questions, even though she denied them at the initial evaluation. In fact, she was perfectionistic at home, had repetitive negative thoughts and she tearfully remarked, "You mean my husband was right when he thought it was strange that I had to have all the shirts buttoned a certain way and put just so in the drawer or I would become very upset?"

Celina then reported rituals that her 8-year-old daughter, Laura, would do before entering a new room, such as running a finger under her nose and licking her lips. Laura also had a locking compulsion. Every time anyone went outside of the house, she would be right behind them, locking the door. Imagine how irritated her brother and sister were because they could never go out of the house to play without being locked out.

I was also seeing Celina's 10-year-old son, Samuel, for attention deficit disorder and oppositional defiant disorder. Samuel's ADD symptoms did not respond to either Ritalin, Dexedrine or Cylert (stimulants used to treat ADD). The mother reported that once Samuel got a thought in his mind, he was unable to let it go. He would follow her around the house for two and ahalf hours asking her the same questions she had already answered. Samuel was also one of the most negative, hostile children I had ever met. Even though his mother was depressed, he defied her, yelled at his sisters andseem to do whatever he could to make the turmoil in the home worse.

Brain SPECT studies were done on both children to see if they would be similar to the mother's study, which might suggest a genetic component to their problems and/or a similar response to treatment. Interestingly, they had the identical finding as their mother of increased activity in the top, middle portion of their frontal lobes (cingulate system). Neither of the children had limbic system findings, and neither of them were clinically depressed.

Based on the SPECT and clinical information, Celina was placed on Prozac to decrease her depression and help lessen her obsessive thinking and compulsive behaviors. She had a dramatically positive response and reported that she was not bothered when things weren't "just so." The scan also convinced her that her condition was at least, in part, biological and not her fault or the result of a weak will, which allowed her to take her medication for a longer period of time.

Additionally, Samuel was started on Prozac and had a similarly positive response. His behavior became much less oppositional and his school performance dramatically improved. He made the honor roll for the first time in his life and was placed in the "Gifted and Talented" program at school the following year.

Initially, Laura refused to take medication and her ritualistic behaviors continued. Approximately eight months later, she agreed to start Prozac and her compulsive behaviors significantly diminished. The family dynamics improved significantly after the mother and Samuel were treated with medication and psychotherapy.

It was clear that the family dynamics in this family operated on many levels and had an interactive quality to them. The mother's depression and obsessive thinking contributed to the anxiety and behavior problems in her children, and the cerebral blood flow abnormalities in the children probably added to their difficult behavior which further stressed the mother.

When I first submitted this family's case study to a medical journal, one of the reviewers said that it was absurd for me to correlate family dynamics to brain studies. I think it is absurd not to. The patterns in our brain have a dramatic effect on how we feel and how we interact with the world.

Brain SPECT studies can be very helpful in the diagnosis and treatment of obsessive-compulsive disorder because of the secretive nature of many compulsive behaviors. As this case illustrates, Celina was being treated for depression and it wasn't until the SPECT findings were reviewed that a history of her obsessive thoughts and compulsive tendencies were discovered.

The Tooth Fairy and the Cingulate System

Brian, age 6, was very excited the night he lost his first tooth. His tooth was secure under his pillow in a special pouch for the Tooth Fairy. In the morning he was ecstatic to find a dollar. All day long, he thought and thought and thought about the Tooth Fairy. He was so happy, in fact, that he secretly pulled out another tooth after school. His mother, who was surprised by the other tooth, went through the Tooth Fairy ritual again. Two days later Brian pulled out a third tooth. The mother started to get worried, because earlier in the day she saw him tugging at the tooth. She told Brian that the Tooth Fairy doesn't come if you pull out your own teeth. She told him not to do it anymore. There was no Tooth Fairy that night. Over the next month, however, Brian couldn't get the thought of the Tooth Fairy out of his head and pulled three more teeth out. The mother brought Brian to see me for an evaluation.

In Brian's family there was a history of alcohol abuse, depression and obsessive-compulsive disorder. Behavioral interventions were not successful in keeping Brian's hands out of his mouth. Additionally, Brian was oppositional and he had trouble at school. The teacher said he "always got stuck on certain thoughts" and could not pay attention to his class work. After several months of individual therapy that was not progressing, I ordered a brain SPECT study to better understand the patterns in Brian's brain. His study revealed marked increased activity in the top, middle portion of his frontal lobes. I put Brian on a low dose of Zoloft (an anti-obsessive antidepressant) and within several weeks the compulsive teeth pulling disappeared and he was more attentive in class.

Chapter 6

IMAGES INTO MYSTICISM
AND EXPERIENCE
The Temporal Lobes

Quote from Grumpy Old Men:

"One day you wake up and realize that you're not 81 anymore. You begin to count the minutes, not the days, and you realize that you're not going to be around. All you have left is the experiences. That's all there is."
94-year-old father to his 68-year-old son

Functions

Dominant Side (usually the left)
- understanding and processing language
- short term memory
- long term memory
- auditory learning
- retrieval of words
- complex memories
- visual and auditory images

Non-dominant Side (usually the right)
- recognizing facial expression
- rhythm
- music.
- visual learning

The only real treasures we have in life are the images we store in the memory banks of our brains. The experiences. The sum of these stored images is responsible for our sense of personal identity and our sense of connectedness to those around us. Our experiences are significant in making us who we are. The temporal lobes, on either side of the brain behind the temples, store memories and images; they store our experiences. They help us define our sense of ourselves. When our temporal lobes function normally, we have a clear sense of who we are, our life situations and the nature of things around us.

On the dominant side of the brain (usually the left side for most people) the temporal lobes are intimately involved with understanding and processing language, short and long term memory, complex memories, the retrieval of language or words, and visual and auditory imagery. Strong feelings of conviction, great insight, and knowing the truth have also been attributed to the temporal lobes. Could there be a religious part of our brain?

The non-dominant temporal lobe (usually the right) is involved with rhythm, music and visual learning. The temporal lobes help us process the world of sight and sound, and give us the language of life. This part of the brain allows us to be stimulated, relaxed, or brought to ecstasy by the experience of great music.

The temporal lobes have been called the "Interpretive Cortex," as it interprets what we hear and integrates it with stored memories to give interpretation or meaning to the incoming information.

Abnormal activity in the temporal lobes can cause a wide variety of symptoms including: abnormal perceptions, hallucinations, amnesia, feelings of deja vu (that you have been somewhere before even though you haven't), ja mais vu (not recognizing familiar places), periods of panic or fear for no particular reason, periods of spaciness or confusion, excessive religiosity, visual distortions, and rage outbursts.

Fyodor Dostoevsky was reported to have bouts of "temporal lobe seizures." He felt his affliction was a "holy experience." His biographer, Rene Fueloep-Miller, quotes Dostoevsky as saying, that his epilepsy "...rouses in me hitherto unsuspected emotions, gives me feelings of magnificence, abundance and eternity." In The Idiot, Dostoevsky writes:

There was always one instant just before the epileptic fit...when suddenly in the midst of sadness, spiritual darkness and oppression, his brain seemed momentarily to catch fire, and in an extraordinary rush, all his vital forces were at their highest tension. The sense of life, the consciousness of self, were multiplied almost ten times at these moments which lasted no longer than a flash of lightning. His mind and his heart were flooded with extraordinary light; all his uneasiness, all his doubts, all his anxieties were relieved at once; they were all resolved in a loft calm, full of serene, harmonious joy and hope, full of reason and ultimate meaning. But these moments, these flashes, were only a premonition of that final second (it was never more than a second) with which the fit began. That second was, of course, unendurable. Thinking of that moment later, when he was well again, he often said to himself that all these gleams and flashes of supreme sensation and consciousness of self, and therefore, also of the highest form of being, were nothing but disease, the violation of the normal state; and if so, it was not at all the highest form of being, but on the contrary must be reckoned the lowest. Yet he came at last to an extreme paradoxical conclusion. "What if it is disease? he decided at last. "What does it matter that it is an abnormal intensity, if the result, if the sensation, remembered and analyzed afterwards in health, turns out to be the acme of harmony and beauty, and gives a feeling, unknown and undivined till then, of completeness, of proportion, of reconciliation, and of startled prayerful merging with the highest synthesis of life?"

Lewis Carrol is reported to have "temporal lobe experiences" which were described in the visual distortions of Alice in Alice in Wonderland.

Problems

- abnormal perceptions
- hallucinations
- amnesia
- feelings of deja vu
- ja mais vu
- periods of panic or fear for no particular reason
- periods of spaciness or confusion
- excessive religiosity
- visual distortions
- rage outbursts
- headaches or abdominal pain without a clear explanation
- seizures

Seven-year-old Brian became very upset when his mother read "Alice In Wonderland." He said that he felt like Alice. "I have weird things happen to me," he told her. "I see things." During the day he saw objects change shapes, often getting smaller. He also saw green, shadowy ghosts at night. Frightened that Brian was losing his mind (a cousin had been diagnosed with a "schizophrenic-like" illness) his mother brought him to see me. On hearing of these symptoms, I suspected that one or both of his temporal lobes was acting up. His brain SPECT confirmed abnormalities in his right temporal lobe and he was placed on Depakote (an anti-seizure medication effective in the temporal lobes). Within two weeks, Brian's strange experiences disappeared.

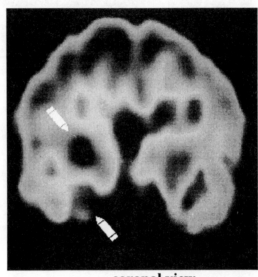

coronal view
note hot and cold areas in the right temporal lobe

Ellen and Jack had similar histories: both had been somewhat reclusive; both had periods of spaciness; and both had periods of panic for no particular reason. Both had religious experiences which occupied a good deal of their lives. Ellen, age 32, was nearly paralyzed by these religious experiences, feeling that they had deep meaning for her. She was unable to work and socially isolated herself. Jack took great interest in these periods of "deep spiritual awakening," but was never able to make out what they meant. Ellen was brought to my office by her parents who were concerned with the social isolation. Jack wanted an evaluation for the panic attacks. Their SPECT studies revealed marked increased activity in the deep aspects of their temporal lobes. The majority of the symptoms for Ellen and Jack went away on Depakote. Even with taking Depakote, both remained deeply religious people, but they were not preoccupied with their thoughts.

Like Ellen and Jack, Jim was bothered by periods of spaciness and panic. He also had periods of "religious thoughts," but they were different. He felt the "presence of the devil" and he was unsure and afraid. The "presence of the devil" haunted him, kept him reclusive from others, and caused him to appear paranoid to his family. Their was a difference between Jim's SPECT study and Ellen's and Jack's studies. Jim's study revealed abnormal activity in the left temporal lobe, rather than the right. In my experience left sided temporal lobe problems are often associated with very negative or "dark" thoughts. After Jim was placed on Depakote, the "presence of the devil" was gone. Several years later, he doesn't like to talk about how he used to feel; he's just very happy he doesn't have those feelings anymore.

Chapter 7

IMAGES INTO VIOLENCE TOWARD SELF AND OTHERS

Violence is a complex human behavior. There has long been a passionate debate over whether or not violent behavior is the result of psychological, social, or biological factors. Current research indicates that violence is, in fact, the result of a combination of all these factors.

Due to the lack of specific biological studies to evaluate violent behavior, clinicians have had to rely on family history to look for genetic factors, along with a history of head trauma, seizures, or drug abuse to evaluate possible medical causes. One of the reasons underlying the lack of clear biological diagnostic tools in violence may be the diversity and variability of the reported findings in the medical literature. Nonspecific and conflicting EEG findings have been reported. A wide variety of neurotransmitter abnormalities have been reported, including disturbances of norepinephrine, dopamine, serotonin, acetylcholine and gamma-aminobutyric acid (GABA). Numerous neuroanatomical sites have also been implicated in violence, including the limbic system, temporal lobes, frontal lobe lesions and prefrontal cortex.

Brain SPECT imaging provides a useful window into the brain of violent or aggressive patients and helps bring together the diversity of biological findings. I have studied several hundred children, teenagers, and adults who exhibited violent or aggressive and compared them to people who have never been violent.

The brain of the violent patient is different than that of the nonviolent person. I have found clinically and statistically significant differences between the aggressive group and the non-aggressive group. The findings clustered around three major findings: decreased activity in the prefrontal cortex, increased activity in the top, middle portions of the frontal lobes (cingulate), and increased activity in the left temporal lobe. Other significant findings included increased focal activity in the left basal ganglia and on the left side of the limbic system.

The brain SPECT profile of the violent or aggressive patient that is suggested by these findings are:

- decreased activity in the prefrontal cortices (trouble thinking),

- increased activity in the top middle portions of the frontal lobes, cingulate gyrus (trouble getting stuck on thoughts),

- focal increased activity in the basal ganglia and/or limbic system (anxiety and moodiness)

- focal increased activity in the left temporal lobe (short fuse).

Case Histories

Paul

Paul, a 28 year old gardener, came to my clinic for work-related problems. He had increasingly intense feelings of rage toward his boss. Paul said that his boss was prejudiced against him because he was Hispanic. He frequently thought about killing his boss. He reported that only the thought of his wife and small daughter prevented him from doing physical harm to his boss. He needed to maintain his job in order to support his family. Paul could not get the anger toward his boss out of his head.

He reported that since childhood he had many explosive outbursts. He saw himself as someday being on the top of a tower shooting down at people. His anger was diffuse. He described having an extremely short fuse, especially while driving. At the age of 7 he ran full speed into a metal basketball pole and was unconscious for several minutes.

Paul had no evidence of a psychotic disorder or a significant depression, although he did complain of short periods of confusion, fear for no reason and episodes of deja vu. His EEG was within normal limits. A brain SPECT study was obtained in order to further evaluate any underlying brain abnormalities that might have been contributing to his difficulties.

Paul's brain SPECT study was significantly abnormal. It revealed normal activity in the prefrontal cortex at rest that worsened when he tried to concentrate (problems with impulsivity). There was also moderate increased activity in the left side of the basal ganglia (anxiety) and an irregular area of marked increased uptake in the deep aspects of the left temporal lobe (short fuse).

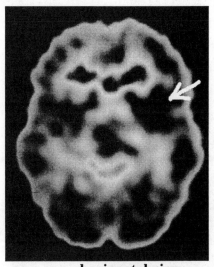

horizontal view
notice increase activity in deep left temporal lobe (arrow)

Because of the clinical picture and information from the brain SPECT study Paul was placed on Tegretol (carbamazepine) at therapeutic levels, along with Prozac several weeks later. After six weeks, he reported that he noted a sense of increased inner control and inner peace. His periods of confusion, deja vu and fearfulness diminished. His anger outbursts decreased and he was able to go to work at a new job.

Steven

Steven, a 39-year-old radio station engineer, was admitted to the hospital for suicidal thoughts. He was recently separated from his wife of eight years. During their relationship there had been mutual physical spousal abuse for which he had spent some time in jail. Steven also complained of having a very "short fuse." He found himself frequently yelling at other drivers on the road and was easily upset at work. On admission he was tearful, had problems sleeping and poor concentration.

He was depressed and experienced with suicidal thoughts. He reported short periods of confusion, periods of feeling intense rage with little provocation, and episodic periods where he would see shadows out of the corners of his eyes. His EEG was within normal limits.

Steven's brain SPECT study revealed marked increased uptake in the deeper aspects of the left temporal lobe and marked increased activity in the cingulate gyrus.

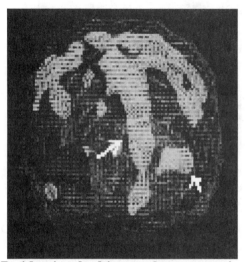

3-D side view looking at the most active areas
marked increased activity in the cingulate gyrus
and deep left temporal lobe

With the clinical picture and information from the brain SPECT it was decided to start Steven on an anticonvulsant in addition to an antidepressant. He was placed on Tegretol at therapeutic levels along with Prozac. Even though he continued to feel sad about the break up of his marriage, he felt calmer, in better self-control and his suicidal thoughts abated. He did report that he wished he would have known about the dysfunction in his temporal lobe years earlier. He felt it may have changed the outcome of his marriage.

Mark

Mark, a 34-year-old corporate employee, was referred by his EAP counselor after he was discharged prematurely from a drug treatment program for psychotic thinking. Mark went voluntarily to the drug program trying to break a ten-year amphetamine addiction. Initially, it was thought Mark had an amphetamine psychosis, but after four months free from any drugs his paranoia and aggressive behavior escalated. On three separate occasions he stormed out of my office, cursing me out each time as he left. He began to display dangerous behavior, expressing homicidal and suicidal ideas along with grandiose thinking. In the past, he had gone through several similar episodes. Mark refused medication, feeling that I might be trying to control or poison him. He did consent to having a brain SPECT study after much encouragement from his family. I ordered the SPECT study because I believed in his fragile state I wouldn't have very many chances at medication and I needed to get to the right medication as soon as possible.

The first time Mark went for his SPECT study he ripped the IV out of his arm and ran from the clinic. He called me an hour later and cursed me out, saying I was trying to poison him. I called his mother, who calmed him down and sat with him through the test.

His brain SPECT study revealed significant decreased uptake in the deep and peripheral aspects of his left temporal lobe.

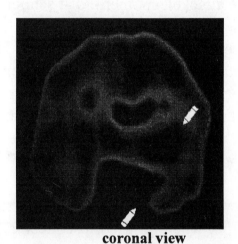
coronal view
note hot and cold areas in the left temporal lobe

With the clinical picture and the SPECT information, Mark was started on an anticonvulsant rather than lithium or an antipsychotic medication. He was placed on Tegretol at therapeutic levels. Within 10 days, he felt calmer and was obviously less paranoid. Within a month, he returned to work at full function and felt more in control of his temper than even before he started using drugs. He was relieved to know about the temporal lobe dysfunction and felt it explained many of the problems he had in the past. He continued his medication without incident.

Kris

Kris was a 12-year-old male with a history of oppositional behavior, emotional outbursts, increased activity level, short attention span, impulsiveness, school problems, frequent lying and aggressive behavior. At age six, Kris was placed on Ritalin for hyperactivity, but it made him more aggressive and it was stopped. He was admitted to a psychiatric hospital in Alaska at age eight for aggressiveness, where he was given the diagnosis of depression and started on an antidepressant, but it had little effect on him.. By the age of 12, a psychoanalyst in the Napa Valley had seen him for several years of psychotherapy, and his parents were seen in collateral sessions as well.

The psychiatrist frequently blamed the mother as the "biggest part of Kris' problem." He told her that if only she would get into psychotherapy and deal with her childhood issues, Kris' problems would go away. Kris' behavior escalated to the point where he was frequently aggressive and uncontrollable at home. He was rehospitalized on the day he attacked another kid at school with a knife.

I was on call the weekend Kris was hospitalized. To bond with the kids, sometimes I play football with them. Kris was on my team. On every single play, he tried to cheat. When we were on defense, he would move the ball back several feet and then turn around to look at me, as if he were trying to get me angry. I refused to play his conflict seeking game, but decided it was time to get a brain SPECT study to help me understand Kris' need for turmoil.

Kris' SPECT study was abnormal. There was a significant left temporal lobe abnormality, in addition, when he tried to concentrate his prefrontal cortex shut down. Kris was placed on Tegretol at a therapeutic level. Within three weeks, he was a dramatically different child. He was more compliant, he was better with the other children on the hospital ward and he was less conflict-seeking with the hospital staff. On the weekend he was being discharged from the hospital, I was again on call. Like the month before, I gathered the kids on the ward and we played football. Kris was on my team. On every single play, he talked to me about what we were going to do. There was no evidence of the prior conflict-seeking behavior. Kris was exhibiting socially effective behavior.

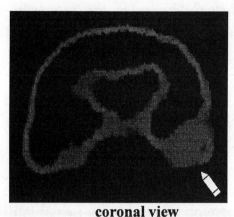

coronal view
note marked cold area in left temporal lobe

After Kris' discharge from the hospital, his mother no longer looked like "the problem." Even though Kris was emotionally more stable, he still had symptoms of attention deficit disorder, having trouble concentrating and following through on his schoolwork. Knowing about the prefrontal cortex drop-off in activity, I added Cylert (a brain stimulant) to the Tegretol, which helped him perform much better in school. Four years after his hospital-ization, Kris is stable and doing well at school and at home. When Kris was 16, I gave a lecture to the faculty at his school. Kris saw me in the parking lot. He ran over to me and gave me a big hug (in front of his friends)! Kris had avoided chronic hospitalizations and therapy because I was able to look into his brain and target the areas that were abnormal.

These findings point to a brain SPECT profile of the aggressive patient that involves specific areas of the brain, especially the left hemisphere. When these findings are taken together, they suggest that aggression is a complex process mediated by several different areas of the brain.

Decreased activity in the prefrontal cortex is a finding often cited in people who are having cognitive difficulty, such as in schizophrenia or major depression. The prefrontal cortex is involved in mediating concentration, impulse control and critical thinking. Aggressive people often misinterpret situations and react in an impulsive manner.

As mentioned above, increased activity in the cingulate is frequently cited as a finding in obsessive-compulsive disorder, a condition where people become "stuck" on certain thoughts or behaviors. Aggressive people often become

93

"stuck" on real or imagined injustices and think about them over and over. For example, in several of the case histories the men often became enraged while driving. They reported that if someone accidentally cut them off on the road they would think and think about it to the point where they would have to do something in order to get the thoughts out of their minds, such as honk, gesture or even chase the person. Studies have shown that medications that increase serotonin in the brain (such as Prozac or Anafranil) normalize activity in this part of the brain.

Increased activity in the basal ganglia is a finding that is often found in patients who are anxious or who have anxiety or panic disorders. People who are aggressive often report a baseline level of tension or anxiety and many clinicians have seen a pattern with these patients where they become increasingly more anxious before they strike out.

Abnormalities in the limbic system have been associated with aggressiveness. Some authors discuss the concept of limbic seizures. Studies consistently find that when a structure termed the amygdala, in the limbic system, is stimulated the person becomes more agitated and aggressive. The limbic system is often cited as the part of the brain that sets the mood. Abnormal activity in this area of the brain may be associated with significant moodiness.

Aggression and abnormalities in the temporal lobes have been described in numerous studies. They are perhaps the most striking finding of my work. Medications such as Tegretol or Depakote have been found helpful in decreasing abnormal activity in this portion of the brain.

In the cases presented, and in my experience with many others, brain SPECT imaging is useful in identifying temporal lobe dysfunction. Traditionally, temporal lobe disorders often go unrecognized in psychiatry because they are difficult to detect with routine EEGs. Yet, they can be associated with fear, memory problems, aggressiveness and altered perceptions such as illusions, deja vu or hallucinations. These areas of abnormalities are often found in the deep structures of the temporal lobes, and are frequently missed by routine EEG studies. In fact, one study demonstrated that during active seizures the EEG was positive in only 21% of cases. Brain SPECT on the other hand, is a more sensitive tool than EEG for the diagnosis and localization of temporal lobe dysfunction.

In my experience with brain SPECT imaging, left-sided brain abnormalities are associated with patients who are more irritable and aggressive. In addition, right-sided brain abnormalities often correlate with patients who are more withdrawn, socially conscious, fearful and much less aggressive.

Andrew

Nine-year-old Andy is my Godson and nephew. He had always been a kind, bright child, who loved Power Rangers, "Nick At Night," and playing soccer and baseball. Over the past year, however, Andy had changed. He had more trouble learning in school. He had become negative, surly, and oppositional. In addition, he had shown aggressive behavior for the first time in his life, getting into many fights at school. In the few months before his parents brought him to see me things began to seriously deteriorate. He went into rages with little or no provocation. On several occasions he became so angry that he broke his own toys. He told his mother that he had thoughts of killing people. He also started talking about killing himself. The final straw occurred when he attacked a little girl on the Little League Field for no apparent reason. This is very abnormal behavior, especially for a prepubertal child. Concerned about his behavior, my brother and sister-in-law brought him from southern California to see me at my office near San Francisco.

As I sat with Andy I felt that there was something different about him. He was more down, more negative than I had ever seen him. As I listened to his parents talk about Andy's scary thoughts and aggressive behavior a number of thoughts went through my mind. Maybe this was a family problem (in my training I was taught a lot about family system theory and how symptoms in one family member often represent stress in the whole family). Maybe Andrew was exhibiting jealous behavior, his brother was a straight A student, a good athlete, and on the outside it appeared the father liked the older brother better (he spent more time with him and was more involved with the sports his brother played).

When I first entertained the idea of getting a SPECT study I questioned myself. Couldn't this just be a psychological or family problem? After all, I could make an argument for pathological family dynamics at work. I had been criticized by other colleagues for ordering these brain studies in children and teens (even though they are easy to do and very safe). Then logic came back to my mind. Nine-year-old children do not normally think about violence, homicide and suicide! Something might be the matter with his brain. Rule out a physical problem first, and if everything is OK then recommend family therapy. I decided to order the brain SPECT scan.

I actually went with Andy to get the brain SPECT scan. He was very brave. He sat perfectly still for the injection of the isotope, and he did his best to lay still during the 15 minutes it took for the SPECT camera to rotate around his head.

When I first looked at the study I thought that there must have been something the matter with the technique of the scan. Andy had a part of his brain missing. As my colleague and I closely looked at the scan, however, we realized that the quality of the scan was excellent. Andy really did have a defect in his left temporal lobe. Nearly two-thirds of this part of his brain was not where it was supposed to be.

The temporal lobes are underneath the temples. They are involved with memory, learning and language. In my clinical experience, abnormalities in the right temporal lobe lead to anxiety, depression and social withdrawal; while abnormalities in the left temporal lobe highly correlate with irritability, aggressiveness, and violence (both toward others and self).

As we looked at Andy's brain we felt that it was critical to order further testing to understand why he had no activity in this part of his brain. Four days later Andy had a brain MRI. Given the SPECT study it was possible that Andy had a tumor, a cyst, a past stroke, or he had experienced severe head trauma (but no one remembered any past head injuries more than the routine bumps and bruises of childhood). Andy's MRI showed a cyst (a fluid filled sack) about the size of a golf ball, pushing against his temporal lobe. The cyst was occupying space where his temporal lobe should be.

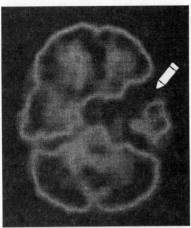
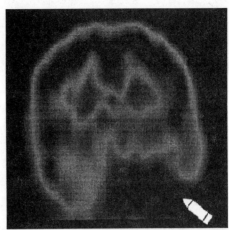

horizontal view   **coronal view**

note area missing in left temporal lobe

As soon as we got the results of the MRI, Andy's family doctor and myself began seeking medical professionals in his area to help with the problem. We talked to five pediatric neurologists in southern California. They all said to leave the cyst alone. They wouldn't operate on him unless he had "real" symptoms, such as headaches, speech problems, double vision, or seizures. They told us that Andy's behavior problems were not in any way related to his brain problem.

In a sad sort of way I had expected that some doctors would react this way. There are still many medical professionals who don't believe that behavior is at all influenced by the physical brain. I even called a renowned pediatric neurologist at Harvard who told me the same thing. They wouldn't operate on him unless he had real symptoms. I was appalled! Suicidal thoughts! Homicidal thoughts! In a nine year old! Give me a break. I kept looking. Finally, I spoke to the chief of pediatric neurosurgery at UCLA. He told me that he had had a patient who was very similar to Andy, a very aggressive teenage boy with a cyst in the same location. The teenager dramatically improved when the cyst was removed.

Andy had his cyst removed at UCLA. It was not easy. The neurosurgeon said that there was serious pressure from the cyst distorting the temporal lobe up into his brain. The cyst had also put pressure on the skull and had actually thinned out the bone under his temple to the point where it was as thin as paper. He told me that if Andy had been hit in the head by a ball at recess it might have fractured his skull! The neurosurgeon went on to say that if he hadn't drained the cyst when he did that within a year Andy would have had what the other doctors were calling "real symptoms," such as speech problems, seizures, and perhaps even death. That comment gave me chills. The neurosurgeon had to go back on two other occasions to drain the cyst and to place a shunt in it to drain excessive fluid that was causing pressure on his brain.

After the cyst was initially drained and the pressure on his left temporal lobe relieved, Andy, once again, was his sweet self. He had no more aggressive behavior, no more violent thoughts, no more suicidal thoughts. Nine months later, he is calm and loving. After Andy woke up from the first surgery, he asked the surgeon if he could take the cyst to school to show his friends. Andy has now taken a great interest in science and wants to be a scientist when he grows up.

I was raised in a strong Catholic family. I was taught to believe that if you live a clean life and work hard you would be successful. I believed that there was something the matter with the character of those people who were drug addicts, murderers, child abusers, and even those who took their own lives. After being involved with about 3,000 brain SPECT studies my mind has completely changed. I now believe that it is essential to evaluate the brain when behavior is out of the bounds of normal. The brain is an organ that dramatically influences behavior, thoughts and feelings. Andy's case was yet another dramatic example to me to press on studying the brains of people with abnormal behavior. What we need is more knowledge, more understanding and less judgment.

Sometimes I cry when I think of all the children and teenagers who are in group homes, residential treatment facilities, juvenile halls, or who have run away from home because their families could not deal with them any longer. I know that many, many of them have brain problems who have never been properly evaluated. Perhaps they have seen a local counselor or physician who looked at the abnormal behavior and told the parents that the child could behave if only he or she really wanted to. In today's "enlightened" society that attitude is as prevalent now as ever. No amount of trying would have changed Andy's behavior.

Even though some naysayers say you really can't see brain abnormalities that correlate with difficult behavior, medicine is developing new tools to look at the brain. I am now more grateful than ever that God has allowed me to be a part of its development.

Here is an example of how these brain problems might impact a family.

Phillip and Dennis

Nine-year-old Phillip was frightened when the police came to his school to talk to him. His teacher had noticed bruises on his legs and arms and she called Child Protective Services. He wasn't sure if he should tell them that his father, Dennis, had beaten him up, or if he should say that he fell down a flight of stairs or something like that. Phillip did not want to get his dad into trouble and he felt responsible for the beating he received. After all, he reasoned, his father had told him ten times to clean his room and for some reason, unknown to Phillip, he didn't do it. Phillip and his father often fought, but it had never been apparent to people outside the home. Phillip decided to tell the truth, hoping that it would help his family get some help.

Indeed, Phillip's family did get help. The court ordered the father to undergo a psychiatric evaluation and counseling for the family. The father was found to have a short fuse and he was impulsive and explosive in many different situations. He began to have problems with aggressiveness after he sustained a head injury in a car accident six years ago. His wife reported that when Phillip was first born, the father was loving, patient and attentive. After the accident, he was irritable, distant and angry.

In family counseling sessions, I noticed that Phillip was a very difficult child. He was restless, active, impulsive and defiant. When his parents told him to stop his annoying behaviors, he just ignored them and continued irritating those around him. I soon discovered it was the interaction between Phillip and his father that was the problem and counseling alone would not be helpful. I believed there was some underlying biological or physical "brain problem" that contributed to the abusive interactions. In an effort to further understand the biology of this family's problems, I ordered brain SPECT studies on Phillip and his father.

The brain SPECT studies for both Phillip and his father were abnormal. The father's study clearly showed an area of increased activity in his left temporal lobe, probably a result from the car accident. Phillip's SPECT study revealed decreased activity in the front part of his brain when he tried to concentrate. This finding, as we have seen, is often found in kids who are impulsive and overly active.

After taking a history, watching the family interact and reviewing the SPECT studies it was clear to me that Phillip and his father's problems were, in part, biological. I placed both of them on medication. The father was put on an anti-seizure medication to calm his left temporal lobe, and Phillip was placed on a stimulant medication to increase activity in the front part of his brain.

Once the underlying biological problems were treated, the family was then able to benefit from psychotherapy and begin to heal the wounds of abuse. In counseling sessions, Phillip was calmer and more attentive, and the father was more able to learn how to deal with Phillip's difficult behavior in a constructive way.

Whenever abuse of a child occurs, it is a severe tragedy. It may become a worse tragedy, however, if people ignore the underlying brain problems that may be contributing to the abuse. In this case and in many others, it is often the interaction between a difficult child and an aggressive, impulsive parent that leads to the problem. These negative interactions may have a biological basis to them. To be effective in helping these families, it is very important to understand the underlying biological or "brain" contribution to the problem.

Suicide

Suicide is the ninth leading cause of death in the United States. It often occurs when a person feels as though he or she has no other option in life. Suicide devastates a family, often leaving parents, spouses, and children feeling abandoned, guilt-stricken, and depressed.

Women attempt suicide three times as often than men. Yet, men actually are successful at killing themselves three times more often than women. In general, the suicide attempts of women are less violent than self-destructive acts of men. Women use drug overdoses, while men are prone to use hanging or guns. Women often use suicide as a cry for help, while men often hold back their feelings until they are overwhelmed and see no other option for healing their pain.

Brain SPECT studies have been useful in helping to further understand suicidal behavior. I have scanned over a hundred people who have had a suicide attempt in their history. They frequently show the violent pattern I described above. The majority of these patients had increased activity in the top, middle portion of their frontal lobes (cingulate -- a tendency to get stuck on negative thoughts), increased activity in the temporal lobes, most commonly on the left side (short fuse and irritability), and decreased activity in the prefrontal cortex during a concentration task (impulsivity and poor judgement).

Most suicidal thoughts are brief in duration. Yet, when someone who gets locked into negative thoughts, also has a short fuse and problems with impulsivity -- watch out! Here are several examples:

Danny

Danny was 8-years-old when his mother brought him to my clinic. He had two recent suicide attempts. He attempted to jump out of a moving car on the freeway, and he put a rope around his neck and tied it to the closet rod. Both times his mother stopped him. She said that Danny wanted to die. He often complained that he hated his life and felt he'd be better off dead. His mother reported that Danny had an obsession with death. At the age of three, Danny fell out of a motor home that was moving about 30 miles per hour. He sustained a head injury with a brief loss of consciousness. Danny experienced a personality change over the next year. He went from being a happy, fun-loving child to a surly, negative, unhappy child. Danny began having monumental temper tantrums. A neurologist had ordered an EEG on Danny when the parents complained he was having periods of spaciness. The EEG was normal. As part of my evaluation, I ordered a brain SPECT study to evaluate why a child so young would exhibit suicidal behavior (very unusual in children under ten).

Danny's SPECT study showed marked increased activity in the deep aspects of his temporal lobes, marked increased activity in the top, middle portion of his frontal lobes, and decreased activity in his prefrontal cortex during a concentration task. No wonder Danny was having so much trouble. Traditionally, play therapy or psychotherapy is the first line of treatment for depressed or suicidal children. Given the seriousness of this case, I placed Danny on Depakote, an anti-seizure medication, to stabilize his abnormal temporal lobe activity. Three weeks later, I added Zoloft to help with his obsessive thinking. Within six weeks, Danny lost the anger in his face, his suicidal thoughts had gone and he was able to interact with his family in a more positive way. Danny was also seen twice weekly in psychotherapy for a few months. Three years later, Danny remains on lowered doses of his medication without any suicidal thoughts.

Mary

Sixteen-year-old Mary was admitted to the hospital for recurrent suicide attempts. This was her fifth psychiatric hospitalization, and she was going to be transferred to a long-term residential treatment facility. Mary also had problems with obsessive thoughts about unusual sexual behaviors, and she compulsively took eight to ten showers a day and changed her clothes that many times during a day as well. Her mother could barely keep up with the laundry. On the day Mary was admitted to the hospital, she had cut her wrists with broken glass. Mary had a paternal uncle who had multiple incarcerations for assaultive behavior. Her father's father was an alcoholic.

Mary's brain SPECT study revealed marked increased activity in the top, middle portion of her frontal lobes, along with increased activity in the left side of her basal ganglia and the left side of her limbic system. The increased activity also spread into the deep aspects of her left temporal lobe. No wonder Mary was in so much pain! Mary had been tried on Prozac in the past, but it made her more aggressive. Given her symptoms and SPECT findings, I put her on Depakote and Anafranil (an anti-obsessive antidepressant). Over the course of the next month, Mary became more relaxed and she was able to talk about her obsessive thoughts. Her suicidal thoughts diminished and it was decided that she could return home rather than go to long-term treatment. She remained in therapy for several years and had no more suicidal attempts. Her SPECT was repeated 8 months later to make sure we were on the right track. There was an 80% decrease in activity in the areas of her brain that were overly active.

Randle

Randle had been hospitalized for two serious suicide attempts before he came to see me. He was the chief executive officer of a computer software company and on the outside it appeared he was a man with everything. He had a beautiful wife, three children, and a successful business. On the inside, however, he was tormented. He often went into rages at home over minor things. He drank too much and he was obsessively jealous whenever any man looked his wife's way. Randle began having a repeat of his suicidal thoughts when he came to see me. Of note, Randle's father had killed himself when Randle was 17-years-old (suicide is often a modeled behavior). His father had been diagnosed as manic-depressive. Randle had an uncle who was an alcoholic, an aunt who was being treated for depression, and a nephew who was on Ritalin for ADD.

On close questioning, Randle said he had "really dark days" even when he wasn't drinking. He also complained of seeing shadows and of frequent spacy periods. I ordered a brain SPECT study to help understand the patterns in Randle's brain. It showed left temporal lobe abnormalities, increased activity in the top, middle portions of his frontal lobes, and decreased activity in his prefrontal cortex when he tried to concentrate. Again, these findings are consistent with a short fuse, obsessive thoughts, and impulsivity. This symptom triad often leads to aggressive behavior, either toward self or others. Randle had a very positive response to a combination of Prozac and Tegretol.

Stalking

In my clinical practice I have studied four people who have been arrested for stalking. All four of these people had the brain pattern I have described for violence with left temporal lobe problems, increased activity in the top, middle portions of the frontal lobes, and decreased activity in the prefrontal cortex in response to a concentration task. These people would get stuck on negative thoughts, such as "I must have her," and they were unable to let go of the thoughts. In three of the four cases, medication helped these men give up their obsessions. The fourth person went to jail. Cheryl was an example of successful treatment.

After seeing an interview on television, Cheryl, 28, became obsessed with a player on a professional baseball team. She started attending every home game. She wrote to him weekly. She couldn't stop thinking about him. She had a responsible job in a bank during the day, but at night and weekends she focused mostly on this one celebrity. When she didn't get any response to her letters she began trying to contact him by telephone and in person. When this was unsuccessful the tone of her letters changed from admiration to irritation and then to subtle threats. After she sent a particularly hostile letter the team reported her to the police. The police warned her to stop trying to contact the ballplayer.

Her brother Peter had been seeing me at the time for obsessive-compulsive disorder. He had a nice response to the combination of Prozac and psychotherapy. When he heard what was going on with his sister he insisted that she come to see me. Reluctantly, she came to my office.

Cheryl was frightened by her own behavior. She had never before had any contact with the police. "I just couldn't get him out of my head," she said. Cheryl had a long history of having trouble getting thoughts out of her head. As a teenager, she had problems with anorexia. As an adult she went through many relationships. Her boyfriends complained that she worried too much and was too jealous. As part of my evaluation of her I ordered a brain SPECT study. It revealed a significantly overactive cingulate. Which is the same finding I found in her brother. As with Peter, Cheryl responded nicely to a combination of an anti-obsessive antidepressant (Prozac) and psychotherapy. She said that the medication allowed her to be more flexible and not get locked into repetitive thoughts.

Chapter 8

HOW DO I GET
THE BRAIN PATTERN
THAT MAKES ME WHO I AM?

Is behavior caused by nature (biology) or nurture (the environment)? Behavioral scientists have been asking that question for centuries. Scientific trends in this area have shifted several times in my own lifetime. Freudian psychoanalysis, psychosurgery, electric shock therapy, hypnosis and the power of suggestion, psychiatric medications and many more therapies have had their followers. The current state-of-the-art in the "nature versus nurture" argument is that both biological factors and environmental factors play a very important role in making us who we are. Let's look briefly at four factors that influence why we do what do: genetics, programming, injuries, and the concept of kindling.

Genetics: Nearly all of the current research suggests that most serious psychiatric disorders (alcoholism, depression, anxiety, ADD, etc.) have genetic or family roots. It is unusual to see someone in my clinical practice who has a psychiatric condition without a clear family history of a similar illness (unless there was a serious trauma, a medical illness or an injury present). In my own family, I have mentioned that my wife and two of my three children have been diagnosed with attention deficit disorder.

I lecture widely to mental health professionals across the country on variety of topics, including all day workshops attention deficit disorder. In the A.D.D. seminar I spend part of the time teaching professionals how to build a successful practice. I tell them that the best way to build an A.D.D. practice is to do a good job. Since this is a genetic disorder, if they do a good job they are likely to have 6 or 7 family members at their doorstep wanting help. In my clinical practice, I have many families where I see multiple members. I have a number of families where I see over 10 other members of the same family, across 3 or even 4 generations.

Programming: Your environment makes a significant difference in how you feel and behave as an adult. The words you hear, the bonds you form, the discipline and direction you were given growing up, all make a difference in your life. We are much more than our biology. They are both important. bipolar disorder (manic-depressive illness) is a good example. From recent studies, we know that bipolar disorder runs in families. Yet, if a person grows up in a chaotic, unpredictable, or abusive home, his or her chances of having early symptoms of the disorder are much higher. For those who have the genetic predisposition for bipolar disorder, but grow up in a stable, loving family, the average age of the onset of symptoms is much later.

Alcohol and drug abuse tendencies are also heavily influenced by both genetics and environment. Studies have shown that adopted children with biological parents who had substance abuse problems are much more likely to have substance abuse problems as adults. Those chances are even greater if these children grow up in a home where alcohol or drugs were abused. Programming and life experiences matter.

Injury: Head injuries, even minor ones, can also have serious impact on behavior. As I presented in the case of Willie in the introduction, a head injury changed the whole way he viewed the world and almost cost another person his life. The brain is very soft. Your skull is very hard. Even minor injuries can cause changes in personality and behavior. One study concluded that up to 70% of people with mild head injuries (dazed but no loss of consciousness) still had symptoms several years later. The symptoms included memory problems, irritability and a drop off in concentration. From the brain studies seenin patients with minor head injuries I have learned that the blood flow patterns in your brain can actually be reset by a head injury. When a person is struck in the forehead, front on, it often causes problems with obsessiveness or worry (injury to the cingulate gyrus. When a person strikes his or her head over the left temple, it can bring on feelings of irritability or violence. When a person has a right-sided brain injury, it is often associated with social withdrawal. Your brain matters. Protect it.

Kindling: Kindling is a neurophysiology term. It is used to describe the properties of a nerve cell during electrical stimulation. I find that the concept of kindling relevant to human behavior and the workings of the mind. Kindling occurs when an electrical current is passed through a nerve cell at a very low voltage. Initially, nothing happens. But as the voltage is raised, eventually the nerve cell will fire off. If there is repeated electrical stimu-lation to the nerve cell at a level that causes it to react, after a time the voltage can be lowered and the nerve cell will continue to fire off. After enough time, the nerve cell will fire off at a very low current of electricity. When this happens the nerve cell is said to be "kindled."

In many ways, our behavior as humans is kindled. For example, if a person grows up in an alcoholic home that is filled with turmoil, and they see constant fighting, their mind becomes kindled to the turmoil. As adults, very little stimulation (a negative look from their partner) may cause them to react in strongly emotional ways. If you were in trouble a lot as a child and frequently scolded or criticized, as an adult you may react very negatively to anyone who even mildly corrects your behavior. Here's an example:

Larry came to my office for an evaluation of attention deficit disorder. He was having trouble organizing and following through with tasks at work. Also, his marriage was on the verge of divorce. His wife said that he was over-reactive to every comment she made. As a child, Larry was hyperactive, restless and impulsive. He was frequently in trouble, both at home and school. He was often in the corner at home, or in the principal's office at school. He had worked very hard to overcome his difficulties and as an adult he owned a very successful business. Due to the level of criticism and failure he experienced growing up, he was overly sensitive to criticism. Anytime his wife said almost anything about his behavior, he reacted angrily against her, feeling attacked. Realizing that he was, in part, reacting out of the pain of the past, helped him to relax a bit in the relationship and not to take everything his wife said as a criticism.

Part 2

Prescriptions For Healing The Mind

In this part of the book I will give specific prescriptions for healing the systems of the mind. These prescriptions are based on my own clinical experience and research, along with an understanding gained from the SPECT studies I have performed on the brain at work. The prescriptions are directed toward helping you overcome the negative mind and behavior patterns that influence your brain function and interfere with your life. The prescriptions are also geared toward helping you optimize the functioning of your brain. The prescriptions include a wide spectrum of behavioral change techniques, and, in some cases medications. By now I'm sure you have an idea which brain patterns seem to apply to you. Focus on the exercises specific to your own needs.

Chapter Nine

ENHANCING FEELING STATES
Limbic System Prescriptions

Finally, brethren, whatever it true,
whatever is honorable,
whatever is right,
whatever is pure,
whatever is lovely,
whatever is of good repute,
if there is any excellence and
if anything worthy of praise,
let your mind dwell on these things.
Phillipians 4:8

Remember that in Chapter 2 we said the limbic system processes the sense of smell, stores highly charged emotional memories, and affects sleep and appetite cycles, moods, sexuality and bonding. To heal limbic system problems we need to focus on a number of things: how the mind/body works, what it is that alters feeling states, the proper management of memories, the connection between pleasant smells and moods, and building positive bonds between oneself and others. The following strategies, geared toward healing limbic system problems, are based on my own personal clinical experience with patients, as well as general knowledge about how the mind/body works.

Limbic Prescription # 1
Kill the ANTs

Our overall mind state has a certain tone or flavor based largely on the types of thoughts we think. When the limbic system is overactive, it sets the mind's filter onto "negative." If you could look into the minds of depressed people, you would find one dispiriting thought following another. When they look at the past, there is regret. When they look at the future there is anxiety and pessimism. In the present moment, something is always unsatisfactory. The lens through which they see themselves, others, and the world has a dim grayness to it. They are suffering from Automatic Negative

Thoughts, or ANTs. ANTs are cynical, gloomy, and complaining thoughts that just seem to keep coming all by themselves.

ANTs can cause people to be depressed and fatalistic, which have a profound impact on their lives. "I know I won't pass that test on Tuesday." This kind of thinking makes for a self-fulfilling prophecy: if they've already convinced themselves they won't pass, they won't study very hard. People who are depressed have a victim mentality. "There wasn't anything I could do about it." They are not pro-active; in other words, instead of taking action to rectify a situation, they don't see themselves in control so it is easier to do nothing and either blame others or blame fate for their failure. Consequently, depressed people often complain a lot. If there is a problem, instead of telling the person who can do something about it, they complain to a third party.

This type of thinking severely limits a person's ability to enjoy his or her life because how one thinks on a moment-to-moment basis plays a large role in how one feels and how one conducts one's affairs. If you are depressed all the time, you don't expect good things tohappen so you don't try very hard to make them happen. The internal distress from melancholy thinking can make you behave in ways that alienate others, thus causing you to isolate yourself. On the other hand, positive thoughts and a positive attitude will help you radiate a sense of well being, making it easier for others to connect with you. Positive thoughts will also help you be more effective in your life. So as you can see, what goes on in your mind all day can determine whether your behavior is self-defeating or self-promoting.

Most people do not understand how important thoughts are. They leave the development of thought patterns to random chance. Unfortunately, they do not even know it is possible to change their thought patterns. Schools teach us what to learn but not how to use our minds in constructive and positive ways. This is a basic flaw in the educational system because if we knew how to use our minds better, we would not only learn more quickly and efficiently, but learning itself would be an activity we would embrace instead of be intimidated by. In fact, there is no formal place in this society where we can be taught how to turn our attention inward and reflect on our way of thinking, or to challenge the very notions that go through our heads. Our thoughts are always with us, yet we seem to place our attention on everything except them. When our minds are burdened with a constant stream of negative thoughts, it can cause a number of limbic problems:

irritability, moodiness, low sex drive, and so on. If we do not change our moment-to-moment thought patterns, we cannot heal our limbic system.

The following are the actual thinking principles I have used in my practice for many years, and I have seen these principles help my patients heal their limbic systems.

The tone of your thoughts is often controlled by your limbic system. When the limbic system is overactive it sets the mind's filter on negative. Depressed people are often bothered by many negative thoughts. The quality of their thoughts, almost automatically, is very negative. Here are some examples:

"You never listen to me."

"Just because we had a good year in business doesn't mean anything."

"You don't like me."

"This situation is not going to work out. I know something bad will happen."

"I feel as though you don't care about me."

"I should have done much better. I'm a failure."

"You're arrogant."

"You're late because you don't care."

"It's your fault."

These thoughts severely limit a person's ability to enjoy his or her life. How you think "moment-by-moment" plays a large role in how you feel (a limbic system function). Negative thoughts cause you to feel internal discomfort or pain and they often cause you to behave in ways that alienate from other people. Hopeful thoughts, on the other hand, influence positive behaviors and lead people to feel good about themselves and be more effective in their day-to-day lives. Hopeful thoughts also are involved in helping people connect with others.

Healing the limbic system requires a person to heal their moment-to-moment thought patterns. Unfortunately, there is no formal place where you are taught to think much about your thoughts or to challenge the notions that go through your head, even though your thoughts are always with you. Most people do not understand how important thoughts are, and leave the development of thought patterns to random chance. Did you know that every thought you have sends electrical signals throughout your brain? Thoughts have actual physical properties. They are real! They have significant influence on every cell in your body. When your mind is burdened with many negative thoughts, it affects your limbic system and causes limbic problems (irritability, moodiness, depression, etc.). Teaching your limbic system to control and direct thoughts in a positive way is one of the most effective ways to help yourself feel better.

Here are the actual step-by-step "thinking" principles that I use in my psychotherapy practice to help my patients heal their limbic systems.

STEP #1

Did you know...Every time you have a thought, your brain releases chemicals. That's how our brain works...

you have a thought,

your brain releases chemicals,

an electrical transmissions goes across your brain and

you become aware of what you're thinking.

Thoughts are real and they have a real impact on how you feel and how you behave.

STEP #2

Every time you have an angry thought, an unkind thought, a sad thought, or a cranky thought, your brain releases negative chemicals that makes your body feel bad (and activate your limbic system). Think about the last time you were mad. How did your body feel? When most people are angry their muscles become tense, their hearts beat faster, their hands start to sweat and they may even begin to feel a little dizzy. Your body reacts to every negative thought you have.

Mark George, M.D., from the National Institutes of Mental Health, demonstrated this phenomena in a elegant study of brain function. He studied the activity of the brain in 10 normal women under three different conditions. He studied these women when they were thinking about happy thoughts, neutral thoughts, and sad thoughts. During the happy thoughts, the women demonstrated a cooling of the limbic system. During the sad thoughts, he noticed a significant increase in limbic system activity.

STEP #3

Every time you have a good thought, a happy thought, a hopeful thought or a kind thought, your brain releases chemicals that make your body feel good (and cools your limbic system). Think about the last time you had a really happy thought. How did you feel inside your body? When most people are happy their muscles relax, their hearts beat slower, their hands become dry and they breathe slower. Your body also reacts to your good thoughts.

STEP #4

Your body reacts to every thought you have. We know this from polygraphs or lie detector tests. During a lie detector test, you are hooked up to some very fancy equipment that measures:

hand temperature,
heart rate,
blood pressure,
breathing rate,
muscle tension and
how much the hands sweat.

The tester then asks you questions, like "Did you do that thing?" If you did the bad thing your body is likely to have a "stress" response and it is likely to react in the following ways:

hands get colder,
heart goes faster,

blood pressure goes up,
breathing gets faster,
muscles get tight and
hands sweat more.

Almost immediately, your body reacts to what you think, whether you say anything or not. Now the opposite is also true. If you did not do the thing they are asking you about it is likely that your body will experience a "relaxation" response and react in the following ways:

hands will become warmer,
heart rate will slow,
blood pressure goes down,
breathing becomes slower and deeper,
muscles become more relaxed and
hands become drier.

Again, almost immediately, your body reacts to what you think. This not only happens when you're asked about telling the truth, your body reacts to every thought you have, whether it is about work, friends, family or anything else.

STEP #5

Thoughts are very powerful. They can make your mind and your body feel good or they can make you feel bad. Every cell in your body is affected by every thought you have. That is why when people get emotionally upset, they actually develop physical symptoms, such as headaches or stomach aches. Some people even think that people who have a lot of negative thoughts are more likely to get cancer. If you can think about good things you will feel better.

Did you know that Abraham Lincoln had periods of serious depression when he was a child and adult? He even thought about killing himself and had some days when he didn't even get out of bed. In his later life, however, he learned to treat his bad feelings with laughter. He became a very good storyteller and loved to tell jokes. He learned that when he laughed, he felt better. Over a hundred years ago, some people knew that thoughts were very important.

Think of your body like an "ecosystem." An ecosystem contains everything in the environment like the water, the land, the cars, the people, the animals, the vegetation, the houses, the landfills, etc. A negative thought is like pollution to your system. Just as pollution in the Los Angeles Basin affects everyone who goes outside, so too do negative thoughts pollute your limbic system, your mind and your body.

STEP #6

Unless you think about your thoughts they are automatic or "they just happen." Since they just happen, they are not necessarily correct. Your thoughts do not always tell you the truth. Sometimes they even lie to you. I once treated a college student who thought he was stupid, because he didn't do well on tests. When his IQ (intelligence level) was tested, however, we discovered that he was close to a genius! You don't have to believe every thought that goes through your head. It's important to think about your thoughts to see if they help you or they hurt you. Unfortunately, if you never challenge your thoughts you just "believe them" as if they were true.

STEP #7

You can train your thoughts to be positive and hopeful or you can just allow them to be negative and upset you. Once you learn about your thoughts, you can chose to think good thoughts and feel good or you can choose to think bad thoughts and feel lousy. That's right, it's up to you! You can learn how to change your thoughts and you can learn to change the way you feel.

One way to learn how to change your thoughts is to notice them when they are negative and talk back to them. If you can correct negative thoughts, you take away their power over you. When you just think a negative thought without challenging it, your mind believes it and your body reacts to it.

STEP #8

As I mentioned above, negative thoughts are mostly automatic or they "just happen." I call these thoughts "Automatic Negative Thoughts. If you take the first letter from each of these words it spells the word ANT. Think of these negative thoughts that invade your mind like ants that bother a couple at a picnic. One negative thought, like one ant at a picnic, is not a big problem. Two or three negative thoughts, like two or three ants at a picnic, become more irritating. Ten or twenty negative thoughts, like ten or twenty ants at a picnic, may cause the couple to pick up and leave the picnic. Whenever you notice these automatic negative thoughts or ANTs you need to crush them or they'll ruin your relationships. One way to crush these ANTs is to write down the negative thoughts and talk back to them. For example, if you think, "My husband never listens to me," write it down and then write down a rational response; something like "He's not listening to me now, maybe he's distracted by something else. He often listens to me." When you write down negative thoughts and talk back to them, you take away their power and help yourself feel better. Some people tell me they have trouble talking back to these negative thoughts because they feel that they are lying to themselves. Initially, they believe that the thoughts that go through their mind are the truth. Remember, thoughts sometimes lie to you. It's important to check them out before you just believe them!

Here are nine different ways that your thoughts lie to you to make situations out to be worse than they really are. Think of these nine ways as different species or types of ANTs (automatic negative thoughts). When you can identify the type of ANT, you begin to take away the power it has over you. I have designated some of these ANTs as red, because these ANTs are particularly harmful to you. Notice and exterminate ANTs whenever possible.

ANT #1: "Always Thinking"

This happens when you think something that happenedwill "always" repeat itself. For example, if your partner is irritable and she gets upset you might think to yourself, "She's always yelling at me," even though she yells only once in a while. But just the thought "She's always yelling at me" is so negative that it makes you feel sad and upset. It activates your limbic system. Whenever you think in words like always, never, no one, every one, every time, everything those are examples of "always" thinking and usually wrong. Here are some examples of "always" thinking:

"He's always putting me down."
"No one will ever call me."
"I'll never get a raise."

"Everyone takes advantage of me."
"You turn away every time I touch you."
"My children never listen to me."

"Always thinking" ANTs are very common. Watch out for them.

ANT #2 (red ANT): "Focusing On The Negative"

This occurs when your thoughts only see the bad in a situation and ignore any of the good parts that might happen. For example, I have treated several professional speakers for depression. After their presentations they had the audience fill out an evaluation form. If 100 of them were returned and 2 of them were terrible, but 90 of them were outstanding, which ones do you think they focused on? Only the negative ones! I taught them to focus on the ones they liked a lot more than the ones they didn't like. It's important to learn from others, but in a balanced, positive way.

Your limbic system can learn a powerful lesson from the Disney movie, "Pollyanna." In the movie, Pollyanna came to live with her aunt after her missionary parents died. Even though she had lost her parents she was able to help many "negative people" with her attitude. She introduced them to the "glad game," to look for things to be glad about in any situation. Her father had taught her this game after she experienced a disappointment. She had always wanted a doll, but her parents never had enough money to buy it for her. Her father sent a request for a second hand doll to his missionary sponsors. By mistake, they sent her a pair of crutches. "What is there to be glad about crutches?" they thought. Then they decided they could be glad because they didn't have to use them. This very simple game changed the attitudes and lives of many people in the movie. Pollyanna especially affected the minister. Before she came to town he preached hellfire and damnation, and he did not seem to be very happy. Pollyanna told him that her father said that the Bible had 800 "Glad Passages," and that if God mentioned being glad that many times, it must be because He wants us to think that way. Focusing on the negative in situations will make you feel bad. Playing the glad game, or looking for the positive will help you feel better.

ANT #3 (red ANT): "Fortune Telling"

This is where you predict the worst possible outcome to a situation. For example, before you discuss an important issue with your partner you predict that he or she won't be interested in what you have to say. Just having this thought will make you feel tense. I call "fortune telling" red ANTs because when you predict bad things you can make them happen. Say you are driving home from work and you predict that the house will be a wreck and no one will be interested in seeing you. By the time you get home you're waiting for a fight. When you see one thing out of place or no one comes running to the door you explode and ruin the rest of the evening. Fortune telling ANTs really hurt your chances for feeling good.

ANT #4 (red ANT): "Mind Reading"

This happens when you believe that you know what another person is thinking even when they haven't told you. Mind reading is a common cause of trouble between people. I tell my wife, "Please don't read my mind, I have enough trouble reading it myself!" You know that you are mind reading when you have thoughts such as, "She's mad at me. He doesn't like me. They were talking about me." I tell people that a negative look from someone else may be nothing more than constipation. You can't read anyone else's mind. Avoid reading anyone's mind. You never know what they are thinking. Even in intimate relationships, you cannot read your partner's mind. When there are things you don't understand, clarify them and stay away from mind reading ANTs. They are very infectious.

ANT #5: "Thinking With Your Feelings"

This occurs when you believe your negative feelings without ever questioning them. Feelings are very complex, and, often based on powerful memories from the past. As I mentioned above, feelings sometimes lie to you. But many people believe their feelings even though they have no evidence for them. "Thinking with your feelings" thoughts usually start with the words "I feel." For example, "I feel like you don't love me. I feel stupid. I feel like a failure. I feel nobody will ever trust me." Whenever you have a strong negative feeling, check it out. Look for the evidence behind the feeling. Do you have real reasons to feel that way? Or, are you feelings based on events or things from the past?

ANT #6: "Guilt Beatings"

Guilt is not a helpful emotion, especially for your limbic system. In fact, guilt often causes you to do those things that you don't want to do. Guilt beatings happen when you think with words like "should, must, ought or have to." Here are some examples: "I ought to spend more time at home. I must spend more time with my kids. I should have sex more often. I have to organize my office." Because of human nature, whenever we think that we "must" do something, no matter what it is, we don't want to do it. Remember the story of Adam and Eve. The only restriction that God put on them when he gave them the Garden of Eden was that they shouldn't eat from the Tree of Knowledge. Almost immediately after God told them what they "shouldn't do" they started to wonder why they shouldn't do it. Well, you know the rest of the story. They ate from the tree and ended up being kicked out of the Garden of Eden. It is better to replace "guilt beatings" with phrases like "I want to do this...It fits my goals to do that...It would be helpful to do this...." So in our examples above, it would be helpful to change those phrases to "I want to spend more time at home. It's in our best interest for my kids and I to spend more time together. I want to please my spouse by making wonderful love with him (or her) because he (or she) is important to me. It's in my best interest to organize my office." Get rid of this unnecessary emotional turbulence that holds you back from achieving the goals you want.

ANT #7: "Labeling"

Whenever you attach a negative label to yourself or to someone else, you stop your ability to take a clear look at the situation. Some examples of negative labels that people use are "jerk, frigid, arrogant and irresponsible." Negative labels are very harmful, because whenever you call yourself or someone else a jerk or arrogant you lump that person in your mind with all of the "jerks" or "arrogant people" that you've ever known and you become unable to deal with them in a reasonable way. Stay away from negative labels.

ANT #8: "Personalization"

Innocuous events are taken to have personal meaning. "My husband boss didn't talk to me this morning. He must be mad at me." Or, one feels he or she is the cause of all the bad things that happen, "My son got into an accident with the car. I should have spent more time teaching him to drive. It must be my fault." There are many other reasons for behavior besides the negative explanations an abnormal limbic system picks out. For example, your husband may not have talked to you because he was preoccupied, upset or in a hurry. You never fully know why people do what they do. Try not to personalize their behavior.

ANT #9 (the most poisonous red ANT): "Blame"

Blame is very harmful. When you blame something or someone else for the problems in your life, you become a victim of circumstances and you cannot do anything to change your situation. Many relationships are ruined by people who blame their partner when things go wrong. They take little responsibility for their problems. When something goes wrong at home or at work, they try to find someone to blame. They rarely admit their own problems. Typically, you'll hear statements from them like:

"It wasn't my fault that...."

"That wouldn't have happened if you had...."

"How was I supposed to know...."

"It's your fault that...."

The bottom line statement goes something like this: "If only you had done something differently, I wouldn't be in the predicament I'm in. It's your fault, and I'm not responsible."

Whenever you blame someone else for the problems in your life, you become powerless to change anything. The "Blame Game" hurts your personal sense of power. Stay away from blaming thoughts and take personal responsibility to change the problems you have.

Summary of A.N.T. Species:

1. "Always" thinking: thinking in words like always, never, no one, every one, every time, everything.

2. Focusing on the negative: only seeing the bad in a situation.

3. Fortune telling: predicting the worst possible outcome to a situation.

4. Mind reading: believing that you know what another person is thinking, even though they haven't told you.

5. Thinking with your feelings: believing negative feelings without ever questioning them.

6. Guilt beatings: thinking in words like "should, must, ought or have to."

7. Labeling: attaching a negative label to yourself or to someone else.

8. Personalization: innocuous events are taken to have personal meaning.

9. Blame: blaming someone else for your own problems.

As we can see, your thoughts really matter. They can either help or hurt your limbic system. Left unchecked, ANTs will cause an infection in your whole body system. Whenever you notice ANTs, you need to crush them or they'll affect your relationships, your work, and your entire life. First you need to notice them. If you can catch them at the moment they occur and correct them, you take away the power they have over you. When a negative thought goes unchallenged, your mind believes it and your body reacts to it.

One way to defeat the ANTs is to write down the negative thoughts that run through your mind, and write down a response that is reasonable, intelligent, and to the point. ANTs have an illogical logic. By bringing them into the open and examining them consciously, you can see for yourself how little sense it really makes to say these kinds of things to yourself. You take back control over your own life instead of leaving your fate to conditioned negative thought patterns.

Sometimes people have trouble talking back to these grossly unpleasant thoughts because they feel that such obvious age-old "truisms" simply must be real. They think that if they don't continue to believe these thoughts they are lying to themselves. Once again, remember that to know what is true and what is not, you have to be conscious of the thoughts and have an intelligent perspective on them. Most negative thinking is automatic and goes unnoticed. You're not really choosing how to respond to your situation, it's being chosen for you, in a way, by habit. To find out what is really true and what is not, you need to question it. Don't believe everything you hear -- even in your own mind!

Limbic Prescription # 2
Surround Yourself with People
Who Provide Positive Bonding

Have you ever picked up a container that had ants crawling on it? Within seconds they are transferred to your body and you are hurriedly trying to brush them off. If you spend a lot of time with negative people, the same thing will happen. You may walk into a room in a buoyant mood, but before long their ANTs are going to rub off on you. Their ANTs will hang out with your ANTs and mate! That's not what you want, so as much as possible, surround yourself with positive people.

Look at your life as it is now. What kind of people are around you? Do they believe in you and make you feel good about yourself or are they constantly putting you down and denigrating your ideas, hopes and dreams? List the five people you spend the most time with. Make a note of how much they support you and the ways in which you would like to be supported more.

In my third year of college I got the bright idea that I wanted to go to medical school. I was, at that time, on the speech team. One day when I was talking to my speech coach I told her about my dream. The first thing out of her mouth was that she had a brother at Michigan State who didn't make it into medical school. "And," she added, "he was much smarter than you are." The message was clear: You don't have a chance. Making a big decision like that was hard enough to do with encouragement; the disheartening comment from the coach was a blow to my confidence I did

123

not need. I went home with my spirits considerably dampened. Later that evening when I told my father what had happened, he just shook his head and said, "Listen, you can do whatever you put your mind to. And if I were you, I wouldn't hang out with that coach."

If you think of life as an obstacle course, it is easy to see that the fewer obstacles in the road, the better it is. Negative people presentunnecessary obstacles for you to overcome because you have to heave your will to succeed, over their doubts and objections and cynicalness. Spending time with people who believe you'll never really amount to anything will dampen your enthusiasm for pursuing your goals and make it difficult to move through life in the direction you want to go. On the other hand, people who instill confidence in you with a can-do attitude, people whose spirits are uplifting, will help breathe life into your plans and dreams.

It cannot be over-emphasized how contagious the attitudes of others are and how much hidden influence they can exert. The reason so many people feel good about attending a positive thinking seminar is that they have been in a room full of people who were all reaffirming the best in each other. But let those people go home and walk into a house where someone makes fun of their efforts and says they're wasting their time and they'll never get anywhere anyway, and watch how fast the positive efforts of the seminar wear off.

When you spend a lot of time with people, you bond with them in certain ways, and as I mentioned earlier, the moods and thoughts of others directly affect the limbic system. If you go out with someone for dinner and after the first half hour you're beginning to feel bad about yourself, and then you remember that you always feel bad about yourself when you have dinner with this person, you are not imagining it; your limbic system is actually being impacted by him or her. Deciding that you don't want to spend time with someone who is going to have an adverse effect on you doesn't mean you have to blame them for the way they are. It simply means that you have the right to choose a better life for yourself.

I believe that limbic bonding is the principle behind the success of support groups like Alcoholics Anonymous. For years, clinicians have known that one of the best ways to help people with serious problems like alcoholism is to get them to connect with others who have the same problem. By seeing how others have learned from their experiences and gotten through tough times in positive ways, alcoholics can find the way out of their own plight. While gaining information about their diseasewas also helpful, forming new relationships and connections with others formed the critical link in the chain of recovery. The same can be said about people with other diseases, like cancer. Stanford psychiatrist David Spiegel demonstrated the effectiveness of support groups for women with breast cancer. Those who participated in a support group had survival rates significantly higher than those who didn't. How our limbic system functions is essential to life itself. Spend time with people who enhance the quality of your limbic system rather than those people who cause it to be inflamed.

Limbic Prescription # 3
Build People Skills To Enhance Limbic Bonds

Enhancing emotional bonds will actually help heal the limbic system, and this has been proven by numerous studies. In one large study in which patients were treated for major depression, the National Institute of Health compared three approaches: antidepressants medication, cognitive therapy (between patient and the therapist involving the way the patient thinks), and interpersonal psychotherapy (between patients). The last of the three worked on enhancing the bonds among the patients themselves. Testers were surprised to find that each of the treatments was equally effective in treating depression; many people in the medical community think that the benefits of medication far outweigh the benefits of therapy. (Not surprising was the fact that combining all three treatments had an even more powerful effect.) So not only were pharmaceuticals and professional therapists helpful, but patients played a significant role in helping each other. How you get along with other people can either help or hurt your limbic system! The more you get along with those around you, the better you will feel.

I teach my patients the following ten principles to help keep their limbic systems (and the limbic system of those they love) healthy and rewarding:

1. Take responsibility for keeping the relationships strong. Don't be the person who blames your partner or your friends for the problems in the relationship. Take responsibility for the relationship and look for what you

can do to improve it. You'll feel empowered and the relationship is likely to improve almost immediately.

2. Never take the relationship for granted. In order for relationships to be special they need constant nurturing. Relationships suffer when they get put low on the priority list of time and attention. Focusing on what you want in a relationship is essential to making it happen.

3. Protect your relationship. A surefire way to doom a relationship is to discount, belittle or degrade the other person. Protect your relationships by building up the other person.

4. Assume the best. Whenever there is a question of motivation or intention, assume the best about the other person. This will help their behavior to actually be more positive.

5. Keep the relationship fresh. When relationships become stale or boring, they become vulnerable to erosion. Stay away from "the same old thing" by looking for new and different ways to add life to your relationships.

6. Notice the good. It's very easy to notice what you do not like about a relationship. That's almost our nature. It takes real effort to notice what you like. When you spend more time noticing the positive aspects of the relationship, you're more likely to see an increase in positive behavior.

7. Communicate clearly. I'm convinced most of the fights people have stem from some form of miscommunication. Take time to really listen and clarify what other people say to you. Don't react to what you think someone means; ask them what they mean and then formulate a response.

8. Maintain and protect trust. So many relationships fall apart after there has been a major violation in trust, such as an affair or other forms of dishonesty. Often hurts in the present, even minor ones, remind us of major traumas in the past and we blow them way out of proportion. Once a violation of trust has occurred, try to understand why it happened.

9. Deal with difficult issues. Whenever you give in to another person to avoid a fight, you give away a little of your power. If you do this over time, you give away a lot of power and begin to resent the relationship. Avoiding conflict in the short run often has devastating long-term effects. In a firm but

kind way stick up for what you know is right. It will help keep the relationship balanced.

10. Time. In our busy lives, time is often the first thing to suffer in our important relationships. Relationships require real time in order to function. Many couples who both work and have children often find themselves growing further apart because they have no time together. When they do get time together, they often realize how much they really do like each other. Make your special relationships a "time investment" and it will pay dividends for years to come.

Limbic Prescription # 4
Recognize the Importance of Physical Contact

The limbic system is not only involved in emotional bonding, it is also involved in physical bonding. Actual physical touching is essential to good health. It would probably surprise some people to know that there are couples who can go for ten years and longer without touching each other. I have seen them in my practice, and they invariably showed such limbic system problems as irritability and depression. It is only after I helped them correct their non-touching behavior that their depressive symptoms improved.

Physical connection is also a critical element in the parent-infant bonding process. The caressing, kissing, sweet words and eye contact from the mother and father give the baby the pleasure, love, trust and security it needs to develop healthy limbic pathways. Then a bond or connectedness between the parents and the baby can begin to grow. Without love and affection, the baby does not develop appropriate limbic connectedness and thus never learns to trust or connect. It feels lonely and insecure, and out of that it grows irritable and unresponsive.

Bonding is a two-way street. A baby, if it's behavior is naturally unresponsive, may inadvertently lessen the amount of love it gets from its parents. The mother and father, misreading the signs, may feel hurt and rejected as if there were something wrong with them as parents and be less encouraged to lavish care and affection on their child. A classic example of this is problem illustrated by autistic children. Psychiatrists used to label the mothers of autistic children "cold"; they believed it was the mother's lack of responsiveness that was causing the autism. In recent times, however, it has been shown in numerous research studies that the mothers started out warm, but actually became more reserved when they did not get positive feedback from their children. The kind of love that is critical to making the parent-infant bond work is reciprocal.

Love between adults is similar. For proper bonding to occur, couples need to hold and kiss each other, say sweet words, and make affectionate eye contact. It is not enough for one side to give and the other to passively receive. Physical manifestations of love need to be reciprocated or the other partner feels hurt and rejected, which ultimately causes the bond to erode.

Intimate relationships really do need love on a physical level in order to flourish. The entire relationship cannot consist of two people sitting in their respective corners having a lively conversation about the stock market (even if they both adore the stock market). An intimate relationship is missing something essential for human beings if there is not enough physical contact. Without that element, eventually love will sour causing one person to withdraw and look for love elsewhere.

Limbic Prescription # 5
Surround Yourself with Great Smells

Your limbic system is the part of your brain that directly processes your sense of smell. That is why perfumes and wonderful smelling soaps are attractive, and unpleasant body odors are repellent. In the British journal Lancet, a study was reported on the benefits of aromatherapy using lavender oil from lavender flowers. When used properly lavender oil aroma helped people to feel less stressed and less depressed. It also enhanced sleep. It has also been reported that the time of day matters as to when they gathered the oil because it was more fragrant at certain times than at others. Aromatherapy puts special fragrances in a steam machine, in the bath, on the pillow, and in potpourris. These fragrances can have an appreciable effect on people's moods. There is a difference between ingesting the substance versus smelling it. When you ingest something it goes to the stomach and gets processed by the digestive system first. A smell, however, activates the olfactory nerves, which go directly to the limbic system.

Another smell encountered in everyday life is cinnamon. Cinnamon is used for cooking in a number of countries throughout the world. I am Lebanese. When I was growing up, my mother used to put cinnamon in many dishes she would bring to the table, including the stuffed grape leaves, which we had all the time. When I recently told her that the scent of cinnamon is considered an aphrodisiac for men, she said she finally figured out why she had seven kids.

Many people have noticed that smells sometimes bring up memories of a particular kind: They are very strong and clear, as if the whole feeling and sense of place of the original event were coming back to them. There is a good reason for that. Smell is processed in the same area of the brain as memories are. Because smells activate neuro-circuits in the limbic system, they bring about a more complete recall of events which gives one access to details of the past with great clarity.

From my long experience in the field, my conjecture is that smells have an effect on moods because the right smells cool the limbic system. While something like depression inflames it, fragrances are like an anti-inflammatory. By surrounding yourself with flowers, fragrances and other pleasant smells, you affect the working of your brain in a powerful and positive way.

Limbic Prescription # 6
Build a Library of Wonderful Memories

Because the limbic system stores highly charged memories, some of the memories are bound to be disturbing. One common therapeutic tool for therapists has been to get clients to scan the past for negative memories so they can reprocess them. Unfortunately, this form of treatment can be misguided, especially for people who are truly depressed. Depressed people have selective memories. They tend only to recall things that are consistent with their mood. Because they have inflamed limbic systems, their mood is negative, and everything they remember is negative. The whole process of recollection makes their lives look like one long bad dream and convinces them that they are justified in being depressed. Therapists sometimes recognize this tendency in clients and put a certain interpretation on it: that the patient is invested somehow in being miserable. But there is another explanation that has to do with how the mind/body works.

Whenever you remember a particular event, your brain releases chemicals similar to those released when you originally input impressions of the event. Consequently, remembering brings back a similar mood and feelings. If the memory is of your puppy getting hit by a car, it will put you in a melancholy mood. People whose bonding with their parents was tentative at best, or who had a lot of painful childhood experiences, already have a chemical imprint on the brain that is negative. They will tend to take in new events in a negative way. Whenever someone looks at them the wrong way, it triggers the same chemical patterns in the brain that are common to their early experience. They also tend to dismiss someone smiling at them and not see it as a positive expression because the puddle their mind is sitting in is not conducive to receiving positive information. Positive information is not consistent with their experience.

This pattern is difficult to change because it sets up a whole way of viewing life: the early patterns continually predispose the people towards taking things in such a way as to prove to themselves that they live in a negative universe. To change the pattern, they actually have to change their brain chemistry by remembering positive things -- even if they have to sit themselves down to do it as an exercise. By calling up pleasant memories, they can tune into mental states that are healthier. The brain then takes on the same chemical patterns that were inputted at the time the healthy events occurred. Because doing this is such a healing process, I encourage those who have lost a loved one to practice it. When someone dies, recalling the fights and the power struggles keeps the pain going because it sets up a mood that is self-perpetuating. By continually remembering the bad things, the emotional filter gets set to actually keep out the good memories. This tends to focus us on the unfinished business instead of the real love that we shared for many years.

For those of us who do not have to battle depression on a daily basis, we may still find ourselves in states more negative than our lives actually warrant. When unfortunate things do happen, we might go on thinking about them for longer than is helpful to solve the problem. In order to balance the bad memories and heal the limbic part of our brain, it is important to remember the times of our life that were charged with positive emotions. Make a list of the ten happiest times in your life. Describe them for yourself in detail, using as many of the five senses as possible. What colors do you remember? What smells were in the air? Was there music? Try to make the picture come alive. In a metaphorical sense you are going through the library shelves of daily experience and looking for the right book.

If you have been involved in a long-term relationship with someone, recollecting the history of your happy times together will enhance the bond between you. Positive memory traces actually encourage behavior that strengthens the bonds. By encouraging affirming thoughts in yourself -- in other words by recalling your partner's caress, how he or she was helpful to you this week, a look or gesture that was particularly touching -- it will tune you into a positive feeling, which in turn will dispose you to act lovingly. It might remind you to call your wife during the day, or to remember what special gift you could give your husband on his birthday that will make him especially happy, or help both of you be supportive when times are tough.

Limbic Prescription # 7
Limbic Medications

Clinical depression, manic-depressive disorder and severe PMS are more severe forms of depression than the garden variety most people experience in the form of bad moods. The limbic strategies I have mentioned so far may not have enough of an effect to help the patient live a happy, functional life. For complete healing to take place, the addition of antidepressant medication may be needed. It has been my experience that a sure sign that the prescribed medications are really treating the depression is that the limbic system activity normalizes. Whenever limbic activity normalizes, there is a corresponding decrease in the patient's symptoms.

In recent years, new antidepressants have entered the market that have a wider application and often have fewer side effects than the original antidepressants. Some of the new pharmaceuticals are important because they have the additional benefit of affecting the subclinical patterns the rest of us are more likely to experience at some time in our lives, such as moodiness and negativity.

For the best results with all my patients, however, I often combine the use of medications with the limbic "strategies" described in this chapter.

Limbic Prescription # 8
Physical Exercise

Physical exercise can be very healing to the limbic system. It releases endorphins that induce a sense of well being. It also increases blood flow throughout the brain, which nourishes it so that it can function properly. Think about what blood flow and nourishment do for the rest of your body. A body that is constricted or emaciated doesn't feel good. The same is true for the brain. Good blood flow resets the limbic system to a healthy level, which in turn favorably affects the person's mood.

People who exercise regularly report a general sense of well being that those who lead a sedentary lifestyle do not experience. They have increased energy and a healthy appetite, they sleep more soundly and are usually in a better mood. Over the years I have found it useful to prescribe physical exercise to depressed patients. This is even more important for people who are unable to tolerate taking antidepressant medication. Instead of taking medication, some are able to treat themselves with a program of strenuous exercise, which made them feel just as good as something from the pharmacy.

In the fast pace of modern life -- long work hours, rush hour commutes, two-parent working families -- it is important to remember how essential exercise and personal care are to good health; don't let them be left out. Technology, in some ways, has worked against us because many of the advances in the past twenty years have reduced and even eliminated physical activity and exertion from our daily lives. In the movie "L.A. Story," Steve Martin runs out of his house, jumps in his car, drives ten yards to his neighbor's house, hops back out and knocks at his neighbor's door. A bit of an exaggeration perhaps, but think of how many times we could walk to the neighborhood store to get a newspaper but we decide to save time to drive. This inactive lifestyle is causing our bodies to lose their efficiency; in other words, they don't burn fat as they should. Experts in nutrition, physiology and medicine all agree that a program of physical exertion on a continuing basis is required to maintain low body fat, a strong and healthy heart, and well toned muscles.

A good exercise program will pay you "limbic" dividends as well:

1. Exercise gives you more energy and keeps you from feeling lethargic.

2. Exercise increases metabolism and will help you keep your appetite in check and, therefore, keep your weight down.

3. Exercise helps to normalize melatonin production in your brain and enhances the sleep cycle.

4. Exercise allows more of the natural amino acid tryptophan to enter into the brain, enhancing mood. Tryptophan is the precursor to the neurotransmitter serotonin, which has been found to be low in many depressed patients. Tryptophan is a relatively small amino acid and it often has to compete with larger amino acids to cross the blood channels into the brain. With exercise, the muscles of the body utilize the larger amino acids and decrease the competition for tryptophan to enter the brain. Exercise makes you feel better.

A lot of people grumble and complain when they're told to get more exercise. They find it time consuming and boring. My advice is to keep trying on different activities until you find the one that suits you. For instance, I found that I hate running, swimming dried out my skin and took too much time, and the stationary bicycle didn't work my upper body enough. Eventually, I discovered that a ski machine was the answer. It was easy to do, it gave me an intense workout in a short period of time, and it was convenient because it was at home. I usually turn up the "Phantom of the Opera" tape and work out to the music, which has the added advantage of keeping up my spirits and adrenaline.

Find out what you like best. But make sure you get some form of regular workout (walking, running, cycling) on a daily basis, and an aerobic workout (which increases your heart rate and the flow of oxygen to your muscles) three times a week for at least twenty minutes a shot. Many people make the mistake of thinking that the sport they play as a hobby fulfills their exercise quota, yet the truth is that it depends on the sport. I once treated an obese man by outlining a nutrition and exercise program for him. Several weeks into it, he complained he wasn't losing any weight. When I asked what kind of workout he was getting, he told me he played two whole rounds of golf a week. I had to point out to him that walking around a golf course would not give him the level of activity he needed because it wasn't continuous -- a golfer has to keep stopping to hit the ball. With a surprised look on his face, he said, "Wait a minute Doc. I don't walk and stop to hit the ball. I get out of the cart, hit the ball, and then get back in the cart. That's a lot of activity, hopping in and out of that cart!"

Limbic Prescription # 9
Limbic Nutrition

Over the past decade there has been significant research on food, nutrients and depression. The results surprise many people. We have been inundated by nutritional experts and news reportswho tell us we should eat low fat, high carbohydrate diets. "Low fat" is everywhere. Unfortunately, low fat is not the complete answer. In two studies in the American Journal of Psychiatry men who had the highest suicide rates had the lowest cholesterol levels. Our limbic system needs fat in order to operate properly. Certainly, some fats are better for us than others, such as omega-3 fatty acids found most prevalently in fish. Protein is also essential to a healthy "limbic diet." Proteins are the building blocks for brain neurotransmitters. Dopamine, serotonin and norepinephrine have all been implicated in depression and mood disorders. It is essential to eat enough protein in balanced amounts with fats and carbohydrates. Too much protein for some people may actually restrict the amount of "brain proteins" to cross into the brain. Not enough protein will leave you with a brain protein deficit. Here are some clues.

Low serotonin levels are often associated with worrying, moodiness, emotional rigidity and irritability (a combination of limbic and cingulate problems). To enhance serotonin levels, eat balanced meals with carbohydrate snacks (such as crackers or bread). Exercise can be a tremendous help along with nutritional supplementation with the amino acid L-tryptophan which was recently re-approved by the Food and Drug Administration and is now available in certain parts of the country. I recommend L-tryptophan in doses of 1,000-3,000 milligrams taken at bedtime. L-tryptophan was taken off the market a number of years ago because one contaminated batch, from one manufacturer caused a rare blood disease and a number of deaths. The L-tryptophan actually had nothing to do with the deaths. L-tryptophan is a naturally occurring amino acid found in milk, meat and eggs. I have found it very helpful for patients to improve sleep, decrease aggressiveness and improve mood control. In addition, it does not have side effects, which is a real advantage over the anti-depressants. There have been some recent studies with Inositol, from the B vitamin family, which you can get from a health food store. In doses of 12-20 milligrams a day it has been shown to decrease moodiness and depression.

Low norepinephrine and dopamine levels are often associated with depression, lethargy, trouble focusing, negativity and mental fuzziness. To enhance norepinephrine and dopamine levels it is better to have protein snacks (such as meat, eggs, or cheese) and to avoid simple carbohydrates, such as bread, pasta, cakes and candy. Also, I often have my patients take natural amino acids such as Tyrosine (1,000-1,500 milligrams a day) for energy, focus, impulsivity and DL-phenylalanine (400 mg three times a day on an empty stomach) for moodiness and irritability.

Chapter 10

REPROGRAMMING ANXIETY AND AVOIDANCE:
Basal Ganglia Prescriptions

The following prescriptions are geared toward healing basal ganglia problems. They are based on what is known about the basal ganglia, as well as personal clinical experience with my patients. Remember, the basal ganglia is involved with integrating feelings and movement, stored patterns and programming from the past, and setting the body's idle or anxiety level.

Basal Ganglia Prescription #1
Understand the Patterns and Triggers
from the Past. Do an autobiography.

The basal ganglia store patterns of learned behavior from the past. As such, in order to properly heal, you must understand the patterns that interfere with your life. This is one of the major goals involved in doing psychotherapy. Many forms of psychotherapy involve making connections with the patterns from he past so that we can be more effective in the present and future. It's often helpful to understand the environment in which you were raised because the "child within" often runs your emotional life. Childhood is the ground where many seeds of emotional reasoning are planted. It provides the base from which we interpret the world. To understand the patterns from the past, I often have my patients write their own autobiography.

The autobiography doesn't have to be long, but must include several important ingredients. Start with writing what you know, good and bad, about your grandparents on both sides (often patterns are passed down for 3 or 4 generations). Next, write down significant memories about your own parents, the good stuff and the bad stuff. Then, starting from birth, from pictures and what you've been told, write down something, good and bad, from each year of your life. Write about times when you experienced the following emotions: sadness, anger, anxiety and despair, along with joy, contentment, excitement and hope. If you put real effort into developing this personal profile, many significant patterns begin to emerge.

Some people begin to see early patterns of self-doubt or self-hatred, which now they can begin to question. Many patients have said to me, "I never liked myself as a kid, but I was just a kid. What could I have done that was so terrible?"

When the autobiography is done with honesty, most people begin to remember some of their mistakes and shortcomings. At this point it's critical to look at whether or not they learn from their mistakes or have a tendency to repeat them.

Emotional connections with the past are the most striking. For example, some people feel a sense of tremendous guilt for things they did as a child or as an adolescent. Yet because the memory is painful they repress the event and only carry around the guilt or shame. Once those events are brought to light and examined, however, the person can then put them into perspective and take away their unconscious, destructive power.

People not only remember difficult times, but they also remember fun and happy times. It's absolutely critical to have and develop positive memories that'll fuel our hope and energy for the future.

Psychologist Abraham Maslow said that information is power. The more information you have about yourself, the more control and direction you'll be able to have over your own life.

Basal Ganglia Prescription #2
Break the Patterns of the Past with Conscious Reprogramming (Self-Hypnosis/Affirmations)

Many of our thought and behavior patterns have been programmed or in a sense "hypnotized" into our minds. When we grow up with many successful experiences, we generally believe we will be successful and act in ways to make that happen. Those who grow up with many failure experiences believe they can't change the problems that are holding them back from being successful in their lives. This negative belief system must change before anything else can.

Appendix A gives a set of instructions to make your own self-hypnotic tape to change the negative emotional messages that may be playing in your head. Make this tape in your own voice, and listen to it everyday. My patients who do this exercise have told me that it is one of the most powerful exercises they have ever done. This tape will help you stay on track toward your goals, as well as give you the positive emotional energy to reach them.

Basal Ganglia Prescription #3
Predict the Best (your beliefs matter).
The expectation of success is a
very powerful force by itself.

People who have basal ganglia problems are often experts at predicting the worst. They have an abundance of Fortune Telling ANTS. Learning to overcome the tendency toward negative predictions is very helpful in healing this part of the brain. Through the years, I have met many people who tell me that they're pessimists. They say that if they expect the worst to happen in a situation, they will never be disappointed. Even though they may never be disappointed, they are likely to die earlier. Your thoughts effect every cell in your body.

Physicians have known for centuries that positive expectations play a crucial role in the outcome of many illnesses. Until one hundred to one hundred and fifty years ago, the history of medical therapeutics was largely that of the doctor-patient relationship and the "placebo effect" (placebos being inert substances that have no physiologic effect on the problem; also called sugar pills, or in Britain, dummy pills). Actually, most of the treatments by physicians back then would have been more harmful than beneficial to the patient. Four of the most famous medications used by physicians until about the eighteenth century were unicorn's horn, used to detect and protect against poisons in wines; benzoar stones, as antidotes for all kinds of poisons; theriac, a mixture of many drugs plus honey, as a universal antidote; and powdered Egyptian mummy, as a universal remedy for almost all ailments, including wound healing. (The unicorn's horn usually came from the ivory of the narwhal or the elephant). Doctors were dangerous to patients. What is surprising, however, is that, in spite of the harmful treatments, many patients, in fact, improved or recovered completely.

The benefits of the placebo effect are determined by the expectations and hopes shared by the patient and the doctor. According to Dr. T. Findley, action, ritual, faith, and enthusiasm are the important ingredients. Jerome Frank, M.D., after studying the psychotherapeutic process, concluded that the belief of the therapist in his treatment and the belief of the patient in the therapist were the most important factors in a positive outcome to therapy.

Although a placebo (expectation) is a substance that is considered pharmacologically inert, it is by no means "nothing." It is a potenttherapeutic tool, on the average about one-half to two-thirds as powerful as morphine in relieving severe pain.

It is clear that our expectations and beliefs have significant impact on our lives. The most effective tool I've found to help people improve their attitudes and increase their expectations is mental rehearsing, or imagineering. I have them imagine themselves reaching their goals with all of their senses. If the goal is increased communication with a spouse, I have them imagine talking to the husband or wife in a way that is conducive to positive communication. If the goal is better sex, I have them imagine it, as they want it, with all their senses. If their goal is to make an outstanding presentation at work, I have them give each step of the presentation in their minds just as they would want to give it.

In sports, mental rehearsing is becoming a standard practice for professional athletes. They imagine themselves making the golf shot, hitting the home run, or intercepting a pass before they walk on the field or right before they hit the ball, step up to the plate, etc. A marathon runner I know said she never thought that she could run a marathon until she heard about mental rehearsing. She tried it, and after six months she ran her first twenty-six-mile marathon. As you believe, so shall you act.

Basal Ganglia Prescription #4
Daily Relaxation, Meditation
and Diaphragmatic Breathing

In order to reset your basal ganglia it is important to set (or reset) it to a relaxed, healthy level. This is best done by a regimen of daily relaxation. Taking 20-30 minutes a day to train relaxation into your body will have many beneficial effects, including decreasing anxiety level, lowering blood pressure, lowering the tension and pain in the muscles, and improving your temperament around others.

Here are several simple relaxation methods that are helpful.

Guided imagery:

Find a quiet place where you can go and be alone for 20-30 minutes everyday. Sit in a comfortable chair (lie down if you won't fall asleep) and train your mind to be quiet. One way to do this is by guided imagery. In your mind's eye, choose your own special haven. I ask my patients, "If you could go anywhere in the world to feel relaxed and content where would you go?" Imagine your special place with all of your senses. See what you want to see there; hear the sounds you'd love to hear there; smell and taste all the fragrances and tastes in the air; and feel what you would want to feel there. The more vivid your imagination, the more you'll be able to let yourself go into the image.

Breathe slowly and deeply, mostly with your belly:

This is one of the main exercises I teach my patients who have panic disorders. I actually write out a panic plan for them to carry with them. On the prescription it say:

Whenever you feel anxious or panicky do the following:

breathe with your belly,

kill the fortune telling ANTs,

try to distract yourself from the feelings,

and if nothing works, take the medication I prescribe for anxiety.

Breathing is a very important part of the prescription. The purpose of breathing is to get oxygen from the air into your body and to blow off waste products such as carbon dioxide. Every cell in your body needs oxygen in order to function. Brain cells are particularly sensitive to oxygen, as they start to die within four minutes when they are deprived of oxygen. Slight changes in oxygen content in the brain can alter the way a person feels and behaves. When a person gets angry, his or her breathing pattern changes almost immediately. Their breathing becomes more shallow and the rate increases significantly. This breathing pattern is inefficient and the oxygen content in the angry person's blood is lowered. Subsequently, there is less oxygen available to a person's brain and they may become more irritable, impulsive and confused, causing them to make bad decisions (such as to yell, threaten or hit another person).

Learn To Breathe Properly

Try this exercise.

Sit in a chair. Get comfortable. Close your eyes. Put one hand on your chest, and one hand on your belly. Then, for several minutes, feel the rhythm of your breathing.

Do you breathe mostly with your chest? Mostly with your belly? Or, with both your chest and belly?

The way you breathe has a huge impact on how you feel moment-by-moment. Have you ever watched a baby breathe? Or a puppy? They breathe almost exclusively with their bellies. They move their upper chest very little in breathing. Yet, most Americans breathe almost totally from the upper part of their chest.

To correct this negative breathing pattern, I teach my patients to become experts at breathing slowly and deeply, mostly with their bellies. In my office, I have some very sophisticated biofeedback equipment that uses strain gauges to measure breathing activity. I place one gauge around a person's chest and a second one around their belly. The biofeedback equipment then measures the movement of the chest and belly as the person breathes in and out. If you expand your belly when you breathe in it allows room for your lungs to inflate downward, increasing the amount of air available to your body. I then teach them to breathe with their bellies by watching their pattern on the computer screen. Over 20 - 30 minutes most people can learn how to change their breathingpatterns , which relaxes them and gives them better control over how they feel and behave.

If you do not have access to sophisticated biofeedback equipment, lie on your back and place a small book on your belly. When you breathe in, make the book go up, and when you breathe out, make the book go down. Shifting the energy of breathing lower in your body will help you feel more relaxed and in better control of yourself.

Meditation:

There are many forms of meditation. They often involve teaching diaphragmatic breathing and guided imagery. Herbert Benson, M.D., in his classic book The Relaxation Response, describes how he had his patients focus on one word, and do nothing but that for a period of time each day. During this time, the patients were to just sit or lie quietly, and only focus on the one word. If other thoughts started to distract them, they were to train their mind to refocus back on that one word. He reported startling results from this simple exercise. His patients reported significant decreases in blood pressure and muscle tension.

Use guided imagery, diaphragmatic breathing, and meditation to reset your basal ganglia and feel more in control of your mind and body.

Basal Ganglia Prescription #5
The 18/40/60 Rule

People with basal ganglia problems often spend their days worrying about what other people think of them. To help them with this problem I teach them the "18/40/60 Rule"

"When you're 18, you worry about what everybody is thinking of you; when you're 40, you don't give a damn about what anybody is thinking of you; and when you're 60, you realize nobody's been thinking about you at all."

People spend their days worrying and thinking about themselves, not you. Think about your day. What have you thought about today? What others (even your partner) are doing or what you have to do or want to do? Odds are you've been thinking about you.

Think about your day. What do you think about? What you have to do that day, who you're going to be with, what your bills are, the headaches your boss or children are giving you, whether or not your spouse will have any affection for you and so on. People think about themselves, not you! You need to base your thoughts and the decisions you make on your goals. Not on your parents' goals, not on your friends' goals, and not on your co-workers' goals.

Worrying about what others think of you is the essence of people who have "social" phobias or those who are fearful or uncomfortable in social situations. The underlying problem is often that these people feel that others are judging them: judging their appearance, their clothes, their conversation and so on.

My patients are amazed to learn that all of the energy they put into worrying about what others think of them is a total waste of energy, energy they could more constructively put into meeting their own goals.

Did you know the most common fear in America, is the fear of public speaking? I have had a number of patients tell me that they failed a class in college because they refused to get up in front of the class and give a speech. That fear was based on how they felt others would judge them or judge their presentation. Often, those who have a fear of public speaking tell themselves that people in the crowd will silently mock them or think bad things about them. The truth is, however, probably some of the people in the audience aren't even listening to their presentation because they are thinking about their anxiety over their own presentation or they're thinking about their own personal problems. The people in the audience who are listening to you, are probably rooting for you to do a good job, because they know from personal experience how hard it is to get up in front of a group of people to speak.

STOP WORRYING ABOUT WHAT OTHERS THINK OF YOU. Base your thoughts, your decisions and your goals on what you want and what is important in your life. Now that is not advocating a self-centered life; most of us want to see ourselves in caring relationships with others and being able to be helpful to others. But you need to base your behavior on what you think, not on what you think others think.

Basal Ganglia Prescription #6
Learn How To Deal With Conflict

As with relationships between countries, peace at any price is often devastating for relationships between people. Many people are so afraid of conflict with others that they do everything they can to avoid any turmoil. This "conflict phobia" actually sets up relationships for more turmoil rather than less.

Here are four typical scenarios of people who fear conflict:

1. In an attempt to be a "loving parent," Sara finds herself always giving in to her four-year-old son's temper tantrums. She is frustrated by how much the tantrums have increased in frequency over the past year. She now feels powerless and gives in just to keep the peace.

2. Billy, a ten-year-old boy was bullied by a bigger ten-year-old named Ryan. Ryan threatened to hurt Billy if he didn't give him his lunch money. To avoid being hurt the Billy spent the year terrified by Ryan.

3. Kelly found herself feeling very distant from her husband Carl. She felt that he always tried to control her and that he treated her like a child. He would complain about what she spent, what she wore and who her friends were. Even though this really bothered Kelly, she said little because she didn't want to fight. However, she found that her interest in sex was nonexistent, she often felt tired and irritable, and that she'd rather spend her free time with her friends than with Carl.

4. Bill worked as the foreman for Chet's company for six years. For most of the past four years Chet became increasingly critical of Bill and belittled him in front of others. For fear of losing his job Bill said nothing, but he became more depressed, started drinking more at home and lost interest in his job.

Whenever we give in to the temper tantrums of a child or allow someone to bully or control us we feel terrible about ourselves. Our self-esteem suffers and the relationship with that other person is damaged. In many ways we teach other people how to treat us by what we tolerate and what we refuse to tolerate. "Conflict phobics" teach other people that it is ok to walk on them, there will be no consequences for misbehavior.

In order to have any personal power in a relationship we must be willing to stand up for ourselves and for what we know is right. This does not mean we have to be mean or nasty, there are rational and kind ways to be firm. But firmness is essential.

Let's look at how the people in each of the four examples could handle their situations in more productive ways that give them more power and more say in their lives.

1. Sara needs to make a rule that whenever her son throws a tantrum to get his way that he will not get what he wants PERIOD. NO EXCEPTIONS. By giving in to his tantrums Sara has taught her son to throw them, which not only hurts his relationship with his mother but will also teach him to be over-demanding with others and hurt his ability to relate socially to others. If Sara can be firm, kind and consistent she'll notice remarkable changes in a short period of time.

2. By giving in to the bully Billy taught Ryan that his intimidating behavior was ok. Standing up to him early, even if it meant being beaten up would have been better than spending a whole year in pain. Almost all bullies pick on people who won't fight back. They use intimidation and are not interested in real conflict.

3. Kelly made a strategic mistake by avoiding conflict early in her relationship with Carl. By giving in to his demands early on she was teaching him it was ok for him to control her. Standing up to him after years of giving in is very difficult, but essential to saving the relationship. I see many, many people who even after years of giving in learn to stand up for

themselves and change their relationship. Sometimes it takes a separation to let the other person know your resolve, but the consequences of being controlled in a marriage are often depression and a lack of sexual desire. Standing up for oneself in a firm yet kind way is often marriage saving.

4. Bill gave up his power when he allowed Chet to belittle him in front of others. No job is worth being tormented by your boss. Yet, most people find that if they respectfully stand up totheir boss that he or she is less likely to walk on them in the future. If, after standing up for yourself in a reasonable way, the boss continues to belittle you then it's time to look for a new job. Being in a job you hate will take off years of your life.

Assertiveness means to express feelings in a firm, yet reasonable way. Assertiveness never equates with becoming mean or aggressive. Here are five rules to help you assert yourself in a healthy manner:

1. Don't give in to the anger of others just because it makes youuncomfortable.

2. Don't allow the opinion of others to control how you feel about yourself. Your opinion, within reason, needs to be the one that counts.

3. Say what you mean and stick up for what you believe is right.

4. Maintain self-control.

5. Be kind, if possible, but above all be firm in your stance.

Remember that we teach others how to treat us. When we give in to their temper tantrums, we teach them that is how to control us. When we assert ourselves in a firm, yet kind way others have more respect for us and treat us accordingly. If you have allowed others to emotionally run over you for a long time they'll be a little resistant to your newfound assertiveness. But stick to it, and you'll help them learn a new way of relating. You'll also help cool down your basal ganglia.

Basal Ganglia Prescription #7
Basal Ganglia Medications

Anti-anxiety medications are often very helpful for severe basal ganglia problems. Nervousness, chronic stress, panic attacks, and muscle tension often respond to medications when the other techniques are ineffective. There are five classes of medication helpful in treating anxiety.

Benzodiazepines are common anti-anxiety medications that have been available for many years. Valium, Xanax, Ativan, Serax, and Tranxene are examples of benzodiazepines. The are several advantages to these medications. They work quickly; they generally have few side effects, and they are very effective. On the negative side, long-term use can cause addiction. In the panic plan I discussed earlier, I often prescribe Xanax as a short-term anti-anxiety medication to use in conjunction with the other basal ganglia prescriptions.

Buspar is a relatively new anti-anxiety medication. It is often very effective in treating long-term anxiety. It also has the benefit of not being addictive. On the negative side, it takes a few weeks to be effective and it must be taken all of the time to be effective. It has shown to have a calming effect on aggressive behavior.

Certain antidepressants, such as Tofranil (imipramine), are especially helpful for people who have panic disorders. I have found these medications to be helpful in patients who have both limbic system and basal ganglia problems.

Focal basal ganglia abnormalities, like focal limbic system changes, are often helped with nerve stabilizing medications, such as Lithium, Tegretol, or Depakote. I have seen these medications be very helpful for some patients.

The last class of medications I find helpful in severe cases of anxiety are anti-psychotic medications, such as Mellaril or Haldol. Because of their side effects, I usually save these medications until I have tried other options. When psychotic symptoms are present, these medications are often lifesaving.

Chapter 11

ACHIEVING TOTAL FOCUS:
Prefrontal Cortex Prescriptions

The prefrontal cortex is the most evolved part of the brain. As such, it is essential in helping you reach your goals. To review, the prefrontal cortex is involved with concentration, attention span, judgement, impulse control and critical thinking. It controls your ability to look at situations, organize your thoughts, plan what you want to do, and carry out your plans. Healing this part of the brain requires the development of a concept I call "total focus."

Prefrontal Cortex Prescription #1
Clear focus on how you want to live.
(THE ONE PAGE MIRACLE)

The prefrontal cortex is involved with concentration, focus, organization, and planning. Developing an ability to keep totally focused in your life will help guide your thoughts and behavior. It will help strengthened the conscious part of your mind.

Here is an exercise I frequently use in my clinical practice to help my patients keep totally focused on what's important in their lives. It is a very healing exercise. I gave it the name of the ONE PAGE MIRACLE because of the wonderful changes I've seen people make in their lives when they can become totally focused on what's really important to them.

On the following page write out what you want for your life in each of the areas listed. Then ask yourself what you are doing to make it happen. After you finish the exercise, put it up where you can see it every day.

Your prefrontal cortex will light up as it looks at this exercise. These are your goals. Make them a part of your mind and soul. Remember that your mind makes happen what it sees.

THE ONE PAGE MIRACLE
What Do I Want?
What Am I Doing To Get What I Want?

RELATIONSHIPS

Spouse/lover:
Children:
Family:
Friends:

WORK

MONEY

SELF

Body:
Interests:
Mind/feelings:
Spiritual:

Prefrontal Cortex Prescription #2
Focus On What You Like a Lot
More Than What You Don't Like

Total focus is one way to keep your prefrontal cortex healthy. Enhance this by noticing what you like about your life and others a lot more than what you don't like. I collect penguins. I have 500 of them in my office. My friends and family have an easy time buying for me at Christmas. In fact, one of my patients saw someone drinking out of a penguin cup, and he talked the person out of that cup to give it to me. Let me tell you why I collect penguins and how they relate to your prefrontal cortex.

I used to live in Hawaii, where there is a place called Sea Life Park. When my son was 7-years-old, I took him to the park to have some special time with him. He wanted to see the penguin show. The penguin's name was Fat Freddie. He did amazing things. He jumped off a 20-foot diving board; he bowled with his nose; he counted with his flippers; he even jumped through a hoop of fire. I had my arm around my son, enjoying the show when the trainer asked Freddie to get something. Freddie went and got it, and he brought it right back. In my mind I thought, "Whoa, I ask this kid to get something for me, and he wants to have a discussion with me for 20 minutes, and then he doesn't want to do it!" I knew my son was smarter than this penguin.

I went up to the trainer afterwards and I asked, "How did you get Freddie to do all these really neat things?" The trainer looked at my son, and then she looked at me and said, "Unlike parents, whenever Freddie does anything close to what I want him to do, I notice him! I give him a hug, and I give him a fish." The light really went on in my head, (even though my son doesn't like fish) whenever my son DID what I wanted him to do, I paid no attention to him, because I was a busy guy, like my own father. However, when he DIDN'T do what I wanted him to do, I gave him a tonof attention because I didn't want to raise a bad kid! I was inadvertently teaching him to be a little monster in order to get my attention. So I collect penguins as a way to remind myself to notice the GOOD things about the people in my life, a lot more than the bad things about the people in my life. If you do that, if you collect something to remind yourself, you'll be much better at focusing your mind and your behavior on what it is you want.

Prefrontal Cortex Prescription #3
Have Meaning, Purpose, Stimulation, and Excitement In Your Life

Have meaning, purpose, stimulation, and excitement in your life to prevent shutdown. Meaning, purpose, stimulation, and excitement are very important in activating your prefrontal cortex. As I mentioned, in my clinical practice I treat many patients who have attention deficit disorder. Short attention span, impulsivity and restlessness characterize this disorder. One of the most interesting parts of the disorder is that there is often an inconsistency of symptoms. For routine, regular, mundane activities, people with ADD often have serious problems. However, when they are engaged in interesting, exciting, stimulating tasks, they often excel. One of the tips I give these patients is to make sure they go into lines of work they love. It can make all the difference between success and chronic failure.

People who have difficulties in this part of the brain often have problems with organization. Learning these organizational skills is often very important. It is also important to know your limitations and, when possible, surround yourself with people who organize you. These people can be intimately involved with your life, such as a spouse or friend, or they can be people who work for you. The most successful people I have seen who have ADD are those people who have others help them with organization. Don't be embarrassed to ask for help. Those people who have ADD who are married to someone who has ADD or who have disorganized office staff find themselves chronically frustrated.

Prefrontal Cortex Prescription #4
Continually Strive To Learn New and Varied Things

Are you learning new things? Are you challenged and stimulated by the world around you? Or, are you bored and waiting to retire or to take a cruise? Many people think of learning as a childhood, teenage or young adult activity. They look forward to the days when they don't have to study anymore, when they know what they need to know. This view of learning, however, causes people to grow old! Learning is certainly one of the fountains of youth. It stimulates healing and growth in the prefrontal cortex.

Dr. Marian Diamond, professor of anatomy at the University of California, Berkeley, reported groundbreaking research on the brain in her book Enriching Heredity. She demonstrated the need for people to remain actively engaged in learning throughout the life cycle. For older people, her research suggested that a person's brain begins to deteriorate when they do not actively use their mind. People who retire and just "putter," along with people who are put in rest homes that provide little stimulation find that their ability to think, concentrate and remember significantly weakens. On the other hand, older people who are actively engaging in learning new things and sharing ideas have sharper mind skills. She gave the example ofan 98 year old university chemist who was still active in writing and research. Getting older does not cause a deterioration in function, Dr. Diamond postulates, a lack of use is the problem. In many ways your brain is like a muscle, the more you use it the stronger it becomes. The less you use it the more it wastes away. The phrase "use it or lose it" applies to your brain. Working and stimulating your brain keeps it young.

Albert Einstein once said that if you study anything for 15 minutes a day you'll be an expert in that field within a year. If you study something for 15 minutes a day for 5 years you'll be a national expert. Fifteen minutes a day is not much time to devote yourself to be a national expert. What interests you? What turns you on? What do you want to be an expert in? It is essential to have your own intellectual pursuits to keep your mind in top physical and emotional condition.

Here are four important keys to learning and intellectual stimulation. I teach my patients these principles, because using them stimulates your prefrontal cortex and makes real change possible.

Be curious. It is the ultimate form of being alive and human. Curiosity is the basis for any learning and keeps you looking for answers in an interested, reflective way.

Ask lots of questions. Formulating the right questionsare critical to finding answers. Many people shy away from asking important questions, because they are embarrassed, worried about what others think of them, and or think they "should know" the answer. Don't be held back by these thoughts, they are not useful. One of the reasons toddlers ask "why" so often is that they don't understand. We need to be the same way and ask "why" until we understand. Always be a student, even when you are teaching. You already know your stuff, why not get the best of what someone else has to offer?

Be observant. Watch yourself and others as you go through your day. Especially keep tabs on the thoughts that go through your head and how you react to others. Real learning comes from observing the world around you.

Think critically. Don't believe something just because someone else said it to you. Look for evidence that makes sense to you. And keep asking why until you understand. Your attitude toward life determines how much you learn. I like the phrase, "When the student is ready, the teacher will appear."

Scientific inquiry is based on these principles. Many people would be surprised to know that they are also essential to psychotherapy. If you can be curious about yourself, ask lots of questions, observe your life as you go through it and think critically, you have a chance at getting what you want out of life and being healthy in the process. Actively seek to stimulate your prefrontal cortex by learning new information.

Beta Brainwave Training

I discussed ADD as primarily a problem in the prefrontal cortex. Medication is the cornerstone of the "biological" treatments for ADD, but it is not the only treatment. Over the past 15 years, Joel Lubar, Ph.D., of the University of Tennessee and other researchers have demonstrated the effectiveness of a powerful new tool in the treatment of ADD. This treatment tool is brainwave or EEG biofeedback.

Biofeedback, in general, is a treatment technique which utilizes instruments to measure physiological responses in a person's body (such as hand temperature, sweat gland activity, breathing rates, heart rates, blood pressure and brain wave patterns). The instruments then feed the information on these body systems to the patient who can then learn how to change them. In brainwave biofeedback, we measure the level of brainwave activity throughout the brain.

There are five types of brainwave patterns:

** delta brainwaves (1-4 cycles per second), which are very slow brainwaves, seen mostly during sleep;

** theta brainwaves (5-7 cycles per second), which are slow brainwaves, seen during daydreaming and twilight states;

** alpha brainwaves (8-12 cycles per second), which are brainwaves seen during relaxed states;

** SMR (sensori-motor rhythm) brainwaves (12-15 cycles per second), which are brainwaves seen during states of focused relaxation

** beta brainwaves (13-24 cycles per second), which are fast brainwaves seen during concentration or mental work states.

In evaluating over 6,000 children with ADHD, Dr. Lubar has found that the basic problem with these children is that they lack the ability to maintain "beta" concentration states for sustained periods of time. He also found that these children have excessive "theta" daydreaming brainwave activity. Dr. Lubar found that through the use of EEG biofeedback, children could be taught to increase the amount of "beta" brainwaves and decrease the amount of "theta" or daydreaming brainwaves.

The basic biofeedback technique has children play games with their minds. The more they can concentrate and produce "beta" states the more rewards they can accrue. On my clinic's EEG biofeedback equipment, for example, a child sits in front of a computer monitor and watches a game screen. If he increases the "beta" activity or decreases the "theta" activity, the game continues. The games stops, however, when they are unable to maintain those brainwave states. Children find the screens fun and we gradually shape their brainwave pattern to a more normal one. From the research, we know that this treatment technique is not an overnight cure. Children often have to do this form of biofeedback for between one to two years.

In my experience with EEG biofeedback and ADD, many people are able to improve their reading skills and decrease their need for medication. Also, EEG biofeedback has helped to decrease impulsivity and aggressiveness. It is a powerful tool, in part, because we are making the patients part of the treatment process by giving them more control over their own physiological processes.

The use of brainwave biofeedback is considered controversial by many clinicians and researchers. More published research needs to be done in order to demonstrate its effectiveness. Also, in some circles EEG biofeedback has been oversold. Some clinics have advertised the ability to cure ADD with biofeedback and without the use of medication. Unfortunately, overselling this treatment technique has hurt its credibility. Still, in my clinical experience, I find EEG biofeedback to be a powerful and exciting treatment and we are yet to see its full development.

Audio-Visual Stimulation

A similar treatment to EEG biofeedback is something called Audio-Visual Stimulation. This technique was developed by Harold Russell, Ph.D. and John Carter, Ph.D., two psychologists at the University of Texas, Galveston. Both Drs. Russell and Carter were involved in the treatment of ADD children with EEG biofeedback. They wanted to develop a treatment technique that could be available to more children.

Based on a concept termed "entrainment," where brainwaves tend to pick up the rhythm in the environment, they develop special glasses and headphones which flashes lights and sounds at a person at specific frequencies which help the brain "tune in" to be more focused. Patients wear these glasses for 30-45 minutes a day.

I have tried this treatment on a number of patients with some encouraging results. One patient, who developed tics on both Ritalin and Dexedrine, tried the glasses for a month. His ADD symptoms significantly improved. When he went off the Audio-Visual Stimulator, his symptoms returned. The symptoms again subsided when he retried the treatment.

I believe that both EEG biofeedback and Audio-Visual Stimulation techniques show promise for the future, but more research is needed.

Prefrontal Cortex Prescription #5
Prefrontal Medication

Medications that help the prefrontal cortex need to be more specifically tailored to the reason behind the underlying problem. Those people who have ADD often respond very well to stimulant medications, such as Ritalin, Dexedrine, or Cylert. I have seen these medications change a person's whole life. These medications work by stimulating the neuro-transmitter dopamine that in turns prevents the prefrontal lobe turnoff that happens in ADD. These medications are safe, well tolerated and make a difference almost immediately.

Several "stimulating" antidepressants are also helpful in ADD. Norpramin (desipramine), Wellbutrin (buprion), and Effexor (venfloxamine) are common ones I use in my practice.

Again, focal abnormalities in this part of the brain seem to respond best to nerve stabilizers, such as Lithium, Tegretol, and Depakote. In addition, I have seen Catapres (clonidine), a blood pressure medication, also have a calming effect on this part of the brain.

Chapter 12

SEEING OPTIONS AND NEW IDEAS:
Cingulate Prescriptions

The cingulate system of the brain allows us to shift our attention from thing to thing, idea to idea, issue to issue. When it is dysfunctional, we have a tendency to get locked into negative thoughts or behaviors; and we have trouble seeing the options in situations. Healing this part of the mind involves training the mind to see options and new ideas.

Throughout this book I have written about the use of medications in healing the brain. I will do so as well in this chapter. It is important to remember, however, that your day-to-day thoughts and behaviors also have a powerful effect on your brain chemistry. UCLA psychiatrist Lewis Baxter demonstrated through award-winning research a powerful mind-body lesson. He studied people who had obsessive-compulsive disorder with PET studies, reporting similar findings to the ones presented in this book. Interestingly, when these patients were treated with anti-obsessive medication, the parts in their brains that were overactive went toward normal activity. This was a revolutionary finding. Medications help heal the functional patterns of the brain. What was more striking, however, was that those patients who were treated without medication, by the use of behavior therapy alone, also showed normalization of the abnormal activity in their brain when the treatment was effective. Changing behavior can also change brain patterns.

Cingulate Prescription # 1
Notice when you're stuck, distract yourself and come back to the problem later

The first step in overcoming cingulate dysfunction is to notice when you are stuck. Becoming aware of the loops of thinking can be very helpful. Keep a log: whenever you find yourself getting locked into a situation, briefly write out what is happening. Notice any triggers that may have set off the thought.

When you find the thoughts "circling the wagons" (going over and over), distract yourself away from them for a bit. Distraction is often a very helpful technique. Here's an example. Maurie, age 32, came to see me for chronic tension. He incessantly worried about his job. He knew that his boss didn't like him, despite getting good performance reviews. The constant worry frequently upset him. He couldn't get these thoughts out of his head. Over and over they went. He complained of headaches, tension, and irritability at home. No amount of rational discussion helped him. I gave him the task of writing down the times he was stuck on these negative thoughts about work. They occurred every several hours. The ANT exercise was helpful for him, but it didn't completely prevent these thoughts from circling in his head. His homework became distraction. Every time one of these thoughts came into his mind he was to sing a song. He picked out several songs he liked and rotated through them, whenever the thoughts started to bother him. This worked for him. He liked the music, and felt as though he had a measure of control over the thoughts that bothered him.

Cingulate Prescription # 2
Don't Try To Convince Someone Else Who Is Stuck, Take a Break and Come Back To Them Later

Don't try to convince someone else who is stuck! If you're locked in the middle of an argument, take a break! Take ten minutes, take ten hours, taken ten days! If you're in a repetitive, negative argument with somebody, and you distract yourself, you're often able to come back later and work it out.

I learned long ago not to try to argue with people who had cingulate system problems. When another person is "stuck" on a thought or behavior, logical reasoning is often ineffective in swaying their opinion. One of the best techniques I've found to deal with those who get stuck is as follows: I will briefly make the point I want to make. If I can tell the other person is getting locked into his or her position, I try to change the subject and distract them away from the topic at the moment. Distraction allows time for the other person's subconscious mind to process what I said without having to lock in on it or fight it. Often, when we come back to the issue, they have a more open mind to the situation. Here's an example:

Jackie came to see me for marital problems. Her husband traveled and was unable to attend many of the sessions. In the individual sessions, I saw that Jackie frequently became locked into her position and left little room for alternative explanations for behavior. Her husband complained of the same thing. He said that she would go on and on for hours and not listen to anything he said. As I realized this was her pattern, I used the brief "attack and retreat" model I described. When she complained about her husband not paying attention to her, I wondered aloud if it wasn't because he felt she didn't listen to his opinion. Immediately, she said I was wrong. She said that she was a very good listener. I didn't argue with her, but went on to something else for a while. The next session, Jackie talked about listening more to her husband. Her subconscious was able to hear what I said, as long as I didn't activate her getting locked into opposing me.

This is often a very helpful technique for teenagers. Many teens argue, just to argue, to oppose their parents. I teach parents to get out of struggles with their teenagers, briefly make their points, and move on to other topics. For important issues, come back to them at later times.

Don't try to convince others who are stuck. Distract them and come back to the point later. This does not mean to give in to someone else just because they are stuck. That will not help. But don't get stuck in an argument with him or her. Take a break.

Cingulate Prescription # 3
Write Out Options and Solutions When You Feel Stuck

Whenever you feel stuck on a thought, it is often helpful to write it down. Writing it down helps to get it out of your head. When you see a thought on paper, it makes it easier to deal with it in a rational way. When these thoughts cause you to have problems sleeping, keep a pen and paper near your bed to write them out.

After you write out a thought that has "gotten stuck," generate a list of the things you can do about it and the things you can't do about it. For example, if you are worried about a situation at work, such as whether or not you'll get the promotion, do the following:

1. Write out the thought. "I'm worried about whether or not I'll get the promotion at work."

2. Make a list of the things I can do about the worry:
"I can do the best job I can at work."
"I will continue to be reliable, hard working, and creative."
"I will make sure the boss knows I desire the promotion."
"In a confident (not bragging) way, I will make sure the boss
   knows about my contributions to the company."

3. Make a list of the things I cannot do about the worry:
"I cannot make the decision for the boss."
"I cannot want the promotion any more than I do."
"I cannot will the promotion to happen. Worrying will not help."
"I cannot make the promotion happen, although I do have lots of
   influence on the process by my attitude and performance."

Use this simple exercise to unlock the thoughts that keep you up nights feeling tense.

Cingulate Prescription # 4
Seek the Counsel of Others When You
Feel Stuck (Often Just Talking About
Feeling Stuck Will Open New Options)

When all of your efforts to rid repetitive thoughts are unsuccessful, it is often helpful to seek the counsel of others. Finding someone to discuss the worries, fears, or repetitive behaviors with can be very helpful. Through the years, I have used mentors to help me through some of the problems I've had to face. Others can be a "sounding board;" they can help you see options; they can be a reality check for you.

Several years after I started performing SPECT studies on my patients, I was professionally attacked by some of the researchers in the field. They tried to discredit my work, even though they never read my work or heard me lecture. I had sent a letter to several of them, asking for their help and collaboration. No response. I was very excited about the clinical usefulness of SPECT in day-to-day clinical practice, and I wanted to

160

share my excitement and newfound knowledge with others. The attack on my work caused me a lot of anxiety and sleepless nights (remember, I have right basal ganglia issues and I have a strong tendency to avoid conflict and confrontation).

I sought the advice of a close friend who had seen the development of my work and who had referred me many patients who had benefited from this technology. When I told him about the attack on my work, he smiled. He then wondered why I had expected anything different. He said, "People who say things that are different used to get burned at the stake." "The more controversy," he continued, "the more of a nerve you're striking in the established community." When I heard him say "what else would you expect," a new way to interpret what had happened was opened. I could look upon the behavior of these other researchers in a new way. In fact, one of the most vocal researchers against my work, who said that I was putting forth ideas that had no scientific basis, himself published findings a year later, reporting what I had seen clinically. When you're stuck, allow others to help you with the process.

Cingulate Prescription # 5
Memorize and Recite the Serenity Prayer Daily
and Whenever Bothered By Repetitive Thoughts

The Serenity Prayer is repeated daily by millions of people around the world, especially those in Twelve Step Programs. It is a beautiful reminder that there are things we can do something about and things we can't do anything about. Many people find it helpful to repeat this prayer in total everyday and every time they are bothered by repetitive negative thoughts. Memorize this prayer (change it as it fits your own beliefs).

God, grant me the serenity
to accept the things I cannot change,
the courage to change the things I can,
and the wisdom to know the difference.
Living one day at a time,
enjoying one moment at a time;
accepting hardship as a pathway to peace,
taking as Jesus did this sinful world as it is,

not as I would have it, trusting that you will make
all things right if I surrender to your will;
so that I may be reasonably happy in this life
and supremely happy with you in the next.
attributed to Reinhold Niebuhr

Cingulate Prescription # 6
Cingulate Medications

As the research has shown, getting stuck on negative thoughts or behaviors is often based on abnormal activity in the cingulate system of the brain. Medications are often very helpful in this part of the brain, especially those medications that increase the neurotransmitter serotonin.

Medications that increase serotonin in the brain are termed serotonergic. These medications include Prozac, Zoloft, Paxil, Anafranil, Effexor, Remeron, Serzone and Luvox. Several research studies have shown that when these medications are effective they normalize activity in the top, middle part of the brain. Clinically, I have seen these medications decrease repetitive thoughts and compulsive behaviors, calm people who overfocus or worry, and relax people who had a tendency to be frozen by their inability to see options. When these medications work, they often have a dramatic effect on thoughts and behaviors.

As with all medications, they do not work all of the time and sometimes they have side effects that can be annoying and even disturbing. Yet, they are the newest weapon in the arsenal against human emotional pain and suffering. They have helped millions of people live more normal lives.

The cingulate system of the brain allows us to shift our attention from thing to thing, idea to idea, issue to issue. When it is dysfunctional, we have a tendency to get locked into negative thoughts or behaviors; and we have trouble seeing the options in situations. Healing this part of the mind involves training the mind to see options and new ideas.

Throughout this book I have written about the use of medications in healing the brain. I will do so as well in this chapter. It is important to remember, however, that your day-to-day thoughts and behaviors also have a powerful effect on your brain chemistry. UCLA psychiatrist Lewis Baxter demonstrated through award-winning research a powerful mind-body lesson. He studied people who had obsessive-compulsive disorder with PET studies, reporting similar findings to the ones presented in this book. Interestingly, when these patients were treated with anti-obsessive medication, the parts in their brains that were overactive went toward normal activity. This was a revolutionary finding. Medications help heal the functional patterns of the brain. What was more striking, however, was that those patients who were treated without medication, by the use of behavior therapy alone, also showed normalization of the abnormal activity in their brain when the treatment was effective. Changing behavior can also change brain patterns.

Chapter 13

ESTABLISHING A LIFE RHYTHM TEMPORAL LOBE PRESCRIPTIONS

In many circles the temporal lobes are still considered a mysterious part of the brain. Yet, they hold two of the keys that make us human. They hold our experiences, and our language and the ability to express to our experiences. It has also been hypothesized that the temporal lobes also contain our religious selves, our ability to look beyond ourselves and connect to the universe around us.

Temporal Lobe Prescription # 1
Strive for Wonderful Experiences

Strive to make your life a series of experiences that keep you motivated, healthy, and excited about your life. As the temporal lobes are the part of your brain which store the experiences of your life, keeping them stimulated with positive experiences will help keep you healthy. Celebrate your life on a regular basis, make your experiences count.

Record the memorable experiences of your life with pictures, videos, diary entries, etc. Develop a library of wonderful experiences. Re-experience them whenever you can. Experiences are your link to life itself. Can it be possible that home movies really are therapeutic? Perhaps not to family and friends, but they certainly are for you.

Temporal Lobe Prescription # 2
Improve Your Ability To Use Words

In addition to storing experiences, the temporal lobes process language. They process the words you hear, and they help you develop your expressions to those around you. Learn as much as you can about the language that you use to relate experiences. Seeing the beauty in words, and learning to express yourself with feeling and creativity can be very therapeutic.

Write your thoughts and experiences in stories, in poetry, in songs. Use new words. Try new language medias. Listen to vocabulary tapes. Keep a dictionary with you to look up new words. Develop your sense of language to optimize and express the experience of your temporal lobes.

Temporal Lobe Prescription # 3
Develop Memory Skills

Memories are stored in the temporal lobes. Most people feel that they are born with their ability to memorize. Memory, however, is clearly a skill that can be enhanced by learning. Here are four simple tools to enhance your memory.

The first of these mnemonics (anything that assists your memory) is a very helpful tool that Loisette wrote about in 1899. The technique provides a simple code for translating numbers into certain letters. This makes it easy to remember any series of numbers by just making up the appropriate words or sentences, using the letters that correspond with the numbers. An example of this system is:

Number	Consonants	Rationale
1	t, d	t has one downstroke, d is a 0+1=1
2	n	n has two downstrokes
3	m	m has three downstrokes
4	r	r is the fourth letter of four
5	l	capital L is the Roman numeral for 50
6	g, j	script g is an upside-down six, and capital J looks like a backward 6

165

7	k, hard c	k can be combined with 7, hard c sounds like k
8	f	both 8 and script f have 2 loops
9	p, b	backward p or upside-down down b is nine
0	z, s	z is the first letter of zero and s looks like a backward z

In this system all other consonants and vowels have no number value. You can master this code in ten minutes or less, and it will be one of the most profitable 600 seconds of your life! You see, you can then translate any number into a word, or sequence of words that can be easily associated in your brain. For instance, if you need to remember the date that Thomas Jefferson first took office as our third president in 1801, then that is easy if you recall Thomas faced a severe test, or T(1) F(8) S(0) T(1), as presidents often do. If you want to remember that your sweetheart's birthday is September 21, think of pant (9-21); the connection should be obvious. And, if you need to remember an important appointment on March 31 at 8:10, recall: Meet me at office at sundown (3-31, 8:10). You can use your keys as the first letter of a series of words, or as all of the keyed letters in a word. Its use in remembering dates, times, and any other numbers is limited only by your imagination.

Second, rhymes are a very popular tool for recalling rules or organization:

"I before E except after C;"

"Spring ahead in Spring, fall back in Fall;"

"Thirty days hath September, April, June and November."

Rhymes help connect items, that otherwise seem totally unrelated, into a metrical pattern. They are very good at establishing definite orders, because any mistake in the order of recall will destroy the rhyme.

The following rhyme aids in retaining a sequence of facts:

One is a bun
two is a shoe,
three is a tree,
four is a door,
five is a hive,
six are sticks,
seven is heaven,
eight is a gate,
nine is a line, and
ten is a hen.

Choose ten facts that you need to remember in a precise order and mentally picture an association between each of them and their corresponding number's object. In less than a few minutes you can easily memorize their order. Try this method with unrelated facts to observe its usefulness to you.

Third, use places to remember specific things. The Greek poet Simonides* was said to have left a banquet just before the roof collapsed and killed all those inside. Even though many bodies were not identifiable, Simonides was able to identify them by their place at the table.

The practical use of this technique involves placing an associative object into a certain location. Then by going back in your mind to the location, the object or fact should come back to you. For example, in memorizing a speech that is organized and outlined, choose the ideas or the major subdivisions and associate them in some way with the different rooms in your home. As you are delivering the speech, imagine yourself walking from room to room discovering the associations you have made in the proper order. If you practice this technique, your associative powers will become limited only by the number of locations you can imagine.

Fourth, the use of acronystic words or phrases (formed from the initial letters of words) can be very helpful. When I have a series of facts to memorize, the first thing I do is to tally their first letters to see if I can arrange them into an associative word or phrase. A few examples of this method include:

"On old Olympus' towering top, a Finn and German viewed a hop." Each first letter corresponds to the first letter of the twelve cranial nerves in their proper order: olfactory, optic, ocular, trochlear, trigeminal, abduceus, facial, acoustic, glossal pharyngeal, vagus, accessory, and hypoglossal.

BRASS is used by marksmen to remember the steps in firing a rifle: breathe, relax, aim, stabilize and squeeze.

The more colorful the acronym, the greater the chance that it will be easily remembered. Go back to the example I used at the beginning of this chapter and review its superb acronymic qualities.

Temporal Lobe Prescription # 4
Sing Whenever/Wherever You Can

Singing in the shower may be healing to your temporal lobes. Song has long been known to have healing qualities.. You can often tell that a person is in a good mood if they are humming or singing. Song is a true joy of life, no matter how you sing. I have seen how the temperaments of my girls change when we sing together. They could be having a terrible day, but when they start singing, often they forget their cares and feel better.

Song has been described as a spiritual experience. When I was in college, I attended Calvary Chapel, a large church in Southern California. The music was incredible. The choir was filled with enthusiasm, which we called "The Spirit of God." I could see how people would become transformed when they started to sing. Shy people would become more involved in the worship; the community glistened with the joy of the music.

Preschool and kindergarten teachers have known for a long time that children learn best through songs. They remember the material easier and it is easier to keep them engaged in the activity. So why do we stop singing in the second or third grade? Perhaps we should continue the singing into later grades.

Interestingly, when I was in basic training in the military, we often sang when we marched. I still have those songs in my head. When we sang as a group, morale went up, and the tasks that we were doing didn't seem quite as bad (like 20-mile road marches).

Sing whenever and wherever you can. You may have to sing softly if your voice is like mine (my 12-year-old daughter is often embarrassed when I sing in church). It will have a healing effect on your temporal lobes, and probably your limbic system as well.

Temporal Lobe Prescription # 5
Listen To a Lot of Music

In a similar way, listen to a lot of great music. Music, from country to jazz, from rock to classical, is one of the true joys of life. Music has many healing properties. Listening to music can activate and stimulate the temporal lobes and bring peace or excitement to your mind.

Music therapy has been a part of psychiatric treatments for centuries. When certain music is played it has a calming effect on patients. Fast-paced, upbeat music has a stimulating effect on depressed patients.

Research has also shown that listening to classical music while studying also has a positive effect on learning. This makes sense if you know the functions of the temporal lobes that are involved in processing music and memory. Certain types of music may activate the temporal lobes and help them learn and process information more efficiently. It is likely that certain types of music open new pathways into the mind.

Certain music can also be very destructive. It is no coincidence that the majority of teenagers who end up being sent to residential treatment facilities or group homes listen to more heavy metal music than other teens. Music that is filled with lyrics of hate and despair encourage those same mind states in developing teens. What your children listen to may hurt them. Teach them to love classical music when they are young.

Listen to music whenever and wherever you can!

Temporal Lobe Prescription # 6
Move In Rhythms.

The temporal lobes are involved with processing and producing rhythms. Many Americans never learn about the concept of rhythm and how important it can be to healing and health. Chanting, dancing, singing, and making love are all forms of rhythms that can be healing.

Chanting is commonly used in eastern religions and orthodox western religions as a way to focus and open one's mind. Chanting has a special rhythm that produces an almost trancelike quality, bringing peace and tranquility to the person. In these states, the mind is more open to new experiences and learning.

Even for people with two left feet like myself, dancing and body movement can be very therapeutic. When I worked on a psychiatric hospital unit, the patients had dance therapy three to four times a week. I often found that my patients were more open and more insightful in psychotherapy after a dance therapy session. Dancing, like song and music, has the ability to change a person's mood and give them experiences they can treasure throughout the day, week, or even longer.

Making love, the rhythmical dance of bodies flowing together, often opens a person's mind to experiences that are beyond words. In the right circumstances, making love is one of the most powerful human experiences.

Look for opportunities to move in rhythms.

Temporal Lobe Prescription # 7
Temporal Lobe Medications

When abnormalities occur in the temporal lobes, serious problems can occur, from seizures to visual changes to abnormal sensory experiences to serious behavior changes. Temporal lobe abnormalities can take away the control you need over your life. Medications can often be very helpful in temporal lobe dysfunction. Depakote (valproic acid) and Tegretol (carbamazepine) are antiseizure medications that are very effective in stabilizing abnormal activity in the temporal lobes. In addition, Dilantin, a classic anti-seizure medication, has also been shown to help in some patients with temporal lobe abnormalities. Although very helpful to your temporal lobes, the prescriptions listed above will not heal seizure activity. If you suspect serious temporal lobe problems, obtain an evaluation by a neurologist or neuropsychiatrist.

Chapter 14

ENHANCING YOUR HUMANITY:
Whole Brain Prescriptions

Through the use of brain SPECT imaging, I've given you a new look into the mind. Using this technology has changed the way I think about people. In my first book, *Don't Shoot Yourself In The Foot*, I took a very strong position advocating personal responsibility, goal setting, and motivation. I believed that if you wanted something bad enough, and you worked hard enough, with the right information, you could be successful at whatever you do. I now know I wasn't telling the whole story. I have learned that your brain matters! The actual physical patterns in your mind have a dramatic impact on how you think, how you feel, and how you interact with the world. Understanding this concept is central to understanding human beings.

Understanding brain patterns does not necessarily mean that all problems are physical, or that they have a genetic nature. Experience and programming, as I have discussed, are also powerful in shaping behavior. To that end, I have given sets of healing exercises for the mind that have included both the judicious use of medication and behavioral change strategies.

I call the last set of prescriptions "Enhancing Your Humanity: Whole Brain Prescriptions." They are not specific to one part of the brain, rather, they involve several brain systems. They're directed at helping you be the best, most effective person you can be. Being effective in life will give you a sense of competence and well-being. These feelings will encourage your brain to release chemicals that help optimize the health of your body and mind.

Whole Brain Prescription #1
Give To Others

Hans Selye, in his book *Stress Without Distress*, coined the term "egoistic altruism." Basically, this term means that when we give to others, it benefits us personally. In the book, I have made the case for the basic human need for "limbic bonding" and social connectedness. In addition, we have a prefrontal cortex need for meaning and purpose. We can optimize our brain function by focusing on helping others.

When we help other people, it does many positive, individual things for ourselves. Helping others makes it easier to put our own problems into perspective. It gives us a sense of importance in the world. It gives us a reason to wake up in the morning. It helps us see beyond ourselves. Helping others, no matter how small, gives us a sense that we matter; that we're important.

I have treated many retirees through the years. When these men or women stop working and just stay home, they often feel lost, frustrated, or bored with their lives. However, when they focus on efforts beyond themselves, for the good of others, they often remain young, vibrant, curious and alive.

I once treated a wealthy 40-year-old mail order entrepreneur. He had made all of the money he could ever spend. He decided to retire, to get out of the daily hassles of the business. For the first year of retirement he stayed home, spending time with his wife. He became more and more restless. He started flying planes, racing cars. It didn't help. He remained restless and unsettled. When he came to see me, he had just had an affair, hoping that would add some excitement to his life. It didn't. He was on the verge of losing his family. He was becoming more and more depressed. Through the therapy, he realized that when he stopped working he had lost a sense of purpose in life. I encouraged him to think about ways he could give back some of his true blessings to others. Initially, he resisted the idea. But the more he thought about it, the more excited he became. He started a non-profit institute to help young entrepreneurs. He loved teaching and being involved with seeing others grow. The more involved he became with others, the better he felt.

Former First Lady Barbara Bush described this phenomena in her life. When she was a young woman she experienced a period of significant depression. To overcome the depression she started to do volunteer work. Helping others made a marked difference in her life and the depression lifted.

Look for ways to be kind and helpful to others. It will make your whole brain feel better.

Whole Brain Prescription # 2
Take Personal Responsibility

Take responsibility for how your life is turning out. Too many people blame others for the problems in their lives and end up as emotional victims of other people. Whenever you blame someone else, you give him or her power over life. You then become dependent on the other person for a solution to the problem. Blaming others can devastate the emotional processes in your brain

Blaming others starts early. I have three children: a son and two daughters. They are all five years apart. When my youngest was 18-months-old, she blamed her older brother, who was 11 at the time, for everything that could possibly go wrong. Her nickname for him was DiDi, and "Didi did it," even if he wasn't home. "Didi did it," and she shouldn't be in trouble.

Blaming others invades every aspect of life. For those of you who watch politics, you know blaming others is rampant. This is clearly one of the reasons our government is often ineffective in solving problems. When you blame other people for how your life is turning out you have no power to change anything. You become a victim, and you cannot do anything about it.

I once treated a woman who came to my office because she was having problems with her boss. She had been in psychotherapy with another psychiatrist for over three years for depression, but seemed to be getting nowhere. She complained that her boss was a sexist and treated her as an inferior person. In our initial interview it was clear that she took no responsibility for how her life was turning out. She blamed her boyfriend for getting her pregnant at age 19 (as if she had nothing to do with it). She then felt "forced" to marry him, but complained that he was unmotivated so she divorced him. Then in succession, she impulsively married two different men who were alcoholics and physically abusive toward her. At the time of our first session she was married to a man who was also an alcoholic and not working. Tearfully, she expressed her feelings of being continually victimized by men, including her current husband and boss.

As I was sitting in my chair listening to what I remember was 45 minutes of blaming other people for how her life was turning out, I turned to her and looked at her and said, "How do you think that you may be contributing to the problems that you have." Now she had seen this psychiatrist for over three years, who had been a well paid listener, who never challenged her. Her mouth dropped open. When she came back the next time, she told me she almost didn't come back saying, "You think it's all my fault, don't you?" I said, "I don't think it's all your fault, but I think you've contributed to your troubles more than you give yourself credit for, and if it's true that you've contributed to your problems then you can do things to change them. As long as you stay an innocent victim of others then there's nothing you can do to help yourself."

Shortly after she started seeing me she began to take a tax course (she hadn't been in college for years). After three or four classes she told me about her lousy teacher. "Oh," I said, "You're setting yourself up to quit the class by blaming the lousy teacher." She said "Oh, I am doing that." Within a couple of weeks she really hung on to the idea, "I'm responsible for how my life turns out." After two years, she graduated from college with a BA and has a good job as an accountant.

When you grow up in a difficult environment, children sometimes are victims of an alcoholic father, or an abusive mother, or a combination of these problems. Some people unconsciously spend the rest of their lives stuck in the mode of being a victim, rather than saying to themselves, "What do I want?" "What am I doing to get what I want?"

Part of having a healthy brain means having attitudes toward life which empower you to be successful. Inventory the areas of your life where you have a tendency to blame other people. Stop blaming them and take responsibility to make a change.

Whole Brain Prescription # 3
Seek Creativity

Creativity is opening your mind. Being creative is having the ability to look at common things in uncommon ways; to take a different approach; to discover our other selves. Creativity does not take genius. It takes an open mind and a willingness to explore all of the options available to you, conventional and nonconventional; and to try new ideas, even when you're not sure if they will work out.

Creativity occurs in all areas of life, not just the arts. We all have the capacity to create newness and change in our worlds when necessary. We only have to take the time to look for new and different ways to approach our lives. Creativity requires looking for new alternatives and new solutions to problems. These new solutions are based on our past experience, current information, and visions for the future.

Relaxation-enhanced Creativity

A relaxed mind is more capable of creative energy than a mind cluttered with the events of the day. Take special time each day to relax, clear your mind, and get beautiful images of where you'd love to be. Once in such a place, ideas and associations will come to you that will help you see things in a different way that is likely to benefit your life. In a way, this relaxing imagery will help you discover the artist that lives within your soul.

To meet this internal artist and creator, go through the following steps.

1. Set aside ten to twenty minutes each day to go through your relaxation exercise.

2. Sit in a comfortable chair, with your feet flat on the floor.

3. Pick a spot on the wall, a little above your eye level. Stare at that spot and count slowly to twenty. As you do this, you'll notice that your eyelids begin to feel heavy and want to close. Let them close.

4. Then imagine yourself floating and drifting to a very comfortable place of your choice. As you go there in your mind, the image will become clear to you. Once there, imagine the place with all your senses. See what is there, hear, feel, smell, and even taste the air of your special place.

5. Next, imagine a very wise person coming toward you. Listen to what he or she tells you. Ask questions, listen for answers. When there are no answers forthcoming, just walk in your special place and enjoy it. Answers will come. Patience may be necessary.

6. After the time you set aside is up, count to three and open your eyes. Tell yourself that you feel relaxed, refreshed, and full of energy to face the rest of the day. Once a week or so, it's a good idea to spend extra time in your special place, just working on ways to look at difficult things in different ways.

If you do this on a regular basis, you'll notice that your general level of tension will decrease, and that you'll have your own special place to look at things differently.

Whole Brain Prescription # 4
Be Teachable

If there is any one secret to success it lies in the ability to get the other person's point of view and see things from his angle as well as your own.
--Henry Ford

Allow your mind to be open to the genius of others. You know what you think. Listen, ask questions, see the situation from someone else's point of view. It will open your mind to new and different ways of thinking.

Have a teachable spirit. Humility basically means that you know you don't know everything, and that you are willing to learn from others. Learning keeps you young. Learning from others keeps you ahead of the field.

Whole Brain Prescription # 5
Learn From Failures.

If I had a formula for bypassing trouble, I wouldn't pass it around. Wouldn't be doing anybody a favor. Trouble creates a capacity to handle it.
                    ---Oliver Wendell Holmes

"A man can fail many times, but he isn't a failure until he begins to blame somebody else."   ---John Burroughs

Abraham Lincoln built a lifetime of accomplishments out of defeats. Look at his record.

He lost his job in 1832.
He was defeated for the legislature in 1832.
He failed in business in 1833.
He was elected to the legislature in 1834.
His sweetheart died in 1835.
He had a nervous breakdown in 1836.
He was defeated for Speaker in 1838.
He was defeated for the nomination for Congress in 1843.
He was elected to Congress in 1846.
He lost the renomination in 1848.
He was rejected for land officer in 1849.
He was defeated for the Senate in 1854.
He was defeated for the nomination for Vice-President in 1856.
He, again, was defeated for the Senate in 1858.
He was elected President in 1860.

Failure is not fatal. Not trying is!

Failure is a part of everyone's life. No one starts out walking in life; it is months before we even learn how to crawl. It is not failure that holds people back, it is their attitude toward failure and their fear of it. Toddlers don't give up when they fall; they take their bruises and try again. Anyone who has had small children knows that despite many failed attempts at mobilization, most children go very quickly from crawling to walking to running to climbing up to places they shouldn't.

It is arrogant to think that we are perfect and we will never fail. We are not programmed with the answers, we learn them. We get the right answers by learning processes and observing our errors along the way. Successful supervisors do not get angry when their employees make mistakes. They say, "Don't be afraid to make mistakes; learn from them. Just don't make the same one twice. Observe what you do and you'll always improve."

How supervisors deal with the mistakes of their employees often determines the quality of the employees. When people go to work and they expect to be yelled at or belittled their fear and anger get in the way of them doing the best they can. When they go to work and know that they will be taught to learn from their mistakes in a positive atmosphere they relax and are more likely to produce good work.

Be a good teacher for yourself and those around you. Maturity is being able to learn from the mistakes you make in a positive atmosphere.

The human brain is expert at learning. It is essential to give it every chance to learn, and not to expect it to know things it hasn't learned. The brain learns best in a positive, relaxed environment. Be kind to yourself. Learn from failures, don't beat yourself up for them.

Whole Brain Prescription # 6
Be a Good Parent To Yourself

The end result of a healthy mind lies in how we treat others and how we treat ourselves. To encourage a healthy mind, I often encourage my patients to be a good parent to themselves. To some people this sounds odd. When we turn 18 we put our parents' authority behind us and, in essence, become our own boss. We make our own decisions, give direction to our lives, and become legally responsible for our actions.

What kind of parent are you to you? Many of the adults I see in my clinical practice are clearly abusive to themselves. They're extremely self-critical, they neglect taking care of themselves and they allow others to dump on them. Carol, a 26-year-old mother of two, was abandoned by her mother when she was 3-years-old. She was subsequently raised partially by her father and by an orphanage. She often felt lonely, even though there were always people around. In raising her own children, she was confused about what was good for them, and had a difficult time disciplining them. Additionally, she was very self-critical, and had trouble pushing herself to do things that were good for her. She often felt depressed.

In therapy with her over several months, we came to the conclusion that she was missing a very important part of herself -- "the good mother." Since her mother had left her early on in life, she was never able to internalize the traits that a protective, nurturing, firm and loving mother gives to her child. She lacked basic self-mothering skills. In helping her to heal she has gone back in her mind to imagine the little girl inside of herself. She began to reparent herself. She often asked herself, "What do little girls need?" And then she started to give those things to herself. For example, she knew that good mothers are firm with their children. So when she had a task to complete, such as the laundry, she did not put it off anymore, she went ahead and did it, which made her feel a sense of relief and accomplishment.

Many people grew up in homes with parents who were overly critical, harsh or neglectful (causing "basal ganglia/programming problems"). As such, a part of themselves have become critical, harsh and neglectful. Those voices and feelings from the past continue to haunt them. How do you treat yourself? How do you treat the child within you? I think that many people need to learn how to reparent the child within themselves to truly heal their minds. Here are seven traits of a "good mother." See if they apply to how you treat yourself.

1. A "good mother" loves her children no matter what. She doesn't always like or approve of what they do, but she always loves them. Do you love yourself no matter what?

2. A "good mother" notices her children when they do things she likes. Her focus is on building self-esteem, rather than tearing it down. When was the last time you noticed something good about yourself?

3. A "good mother" is firm with her children and will push them to do things that are good for them, even if they do not want to do them. She pushes them to do it anyway. Are you good at pushing yourself (in a kind way) to do the things you need done?

4. A "good mother" wants her children to be independent and encourages her children to have choices and make decisions for themselves, under her supervision. Do you feel good about yourself independently of others, or do you depend on the opinion of others to make yourself feel good?

5. A "good mother" helps her children learn from their mistakes. She does not berate them when they make mistakes; rather, she helps them look at what happened, and helps them figure out what to do differently the next time. Do you learn from your mistakes or just beat yourself up when you make them?

6. A "good mother" is not perfect. No one can relate to a perfect person and she is someone who is easy to relate to. Do you expect yourself to be perfect and then beat yourself up when you're not?

7. A "good mother" always notices more good than bad in her children. What do you have a tendency notice about yourself -- good or bad?

When we grow up we become, in a sense, our own parents. How we treat ourselves plays a large role in what we get out of life.

Conclusion:

Your brain matters!

**There may be reasons other than
just simple explanations,
why people act the way they do.**

Use

**limbic,
basal ganglia,
prefrontal cortex,
cingulate,
temporal lobe
and whole brain**

**prescriptions to keep your brain healthy,
strong and working toward your success.**

About the Author

Daniel G. Amen, M.D.

Daniel G. Amen, M.D. is a clinical neuroscientist, psychiatrist and the medical director of a large innovative clinic in Fairfield, California. Dr. Amen is a nationally recognized expert in the fields of "the brain and behavior", self-defeating behavior and attention deficit disorders. He has been the keynote speaker at many national conferences. He has presented his groundbreaking research on brain imaging and behavior across North America. Dr. Amen's clinic has evaluated and treated more than 6,000 people with ADD. In addition, his wife and two of his three children have ADD. He has a deep understanding of this disorder from both a professional and personal perspective.

Dr. Amen did his psychiatric training at Walter Reed Army Medical Center in Washington, D.C. He has won writing and research awards from the American Psychiatric Association, the Menninger Clinic and the U.S. Army.

Dr. Amen has been published around the world. He is the author of over 250 articles, fourteen books, and a number of audio and video programs. His magazine credits include Parade Magazine, Hong Kong Style and American Woman. Dr. Amen has appeared in the media across the country, including television appearances on the Discovery Channel, The Geraldo Show and CNN's Sonya Live, along with over 150 radio appearances. Additionally, Dr. Amen has been quoted by the Wall Street Journal, the Associated Press, the Los Angeles Times and the San Francisco Chronicle.

Keynotes and Seminars by Dr. Amen

IMAGES INTO THE MIND
A Radical New Look At
Understanding and Changing Behavior

WINDOWS INTO THE A.D.D. MIND
Understanding and Treating Attention Deficit
Disorders, Childhood Through Adulthood

FIRESTORMS IN THE BRAIN
An Inside Look At Violent Behavior

DON'T SHOOT YOURSELF IN THE FOOT
A Program To End Self Defeating Behavior Forever

WOULD YOU GIVE 2 MINUTES
A DAY FOR A LIFETIME OF LOVE
A Simple Program To Keep You
Focused On the Love You Need

THE INSTRUCTION MANUAL THAT SHOULD
HAVE COME WITH YOUR CHILD
New Skills for Frazzled Parents

TEN STEPS TO BUILDING
VALUES WITHIN CHILDREN

MINDCOACH FOR KIDS
Teaching Kids to Think Positive and Feel Good

THE SECRETS OF
SUCCESSFUL STUDENTS
How To Be Your Best In School

For information please call (707) 429-7181 or write to:
350 Chadbourne Road, Fairfield, CA 94585

MindWorks Press
Books/Audios/Videos by Daniel G. Amen, M.D.
350 Chadbourne Road, Fairfield, CA 94585
Office 707.429.7181   Fax 707.429.8210
Internet Address http://www.amenclinic.com

WINDOWS INTO THE A.D.D. MIND: Understanding and Treating Attention Deficit Disorders in Children, Teens and Adults
Book: A comprehensive guide to everything you need to know about ADD in children, teenagers, and adults. Includes case studies, diagnostic checklists, subtypes of ADD, brain images, specific suggestions on medication management, individual and family therapy techniques, organizational strategies, and many other ideas for living with ADD at home, school, and work. $29.95____

Brain Train Enhancement Tapes: (2 tapes) Made a special sound machine that produces sound waves at frequencies to help your brain either focus or relax. $29.95____

Self-Hypnosis: (1 tape) Self-hypnotic reprogramming for negative thoughts associated with ADD. $14.95____

Medications For ADD: the latest information on the use of medications for ADD, including the use of combination medications.
Audio $29.95____   Video $49.95

ADD Audio Set: (8 tapes) Live seminar on all aspects of ADD. Also included, "ADD and Medication" tapes, "Brain Train" tapes, and "Self-hypnosis for ADD" tape. $79.95____

Windows Into The ADD Mind Video: (1 hour, 20 min) Dr. Amen LIVE on A.D.D. with personal stories, humor, brain images and practical advice for school, home life, work, and medication. $49.95____

Set Discounts!!   Book/Complete Audios $99.95____   Book/Video $69.95____
                          The Complete Set of Book/Audios/Video $119.95____

A.D.D. IN INTIMATE RELATIONSHIPS
All about the impact and healing of relationships touched by ADD.
Book: $29.95 **Audio:** (2 tapes) $29.95____   **Video:** (90 minutes) $49.95____

A CHILD'S GUIDE TO A.D.D.
Book: A complete guide to A.D.D. for children ages 5-11 in easy to understand language. To be read together by parents and children. $19.95____

A TEENAGER'S GUIDE TO A.D.D.
(Co-authored by 2 teenagers, Antony Amen and Sharon Johnson)
Book: A complete guide for teenagers, including tips on medication, getting along with others at home, school, and work, homework, driving, and relationships. $29.95____
Audio: Dr. Amen and his son Antony present a 90 minute workshop on their book, including the symptoms, along with specific steps for healing. $29.95____
Set Discounts!!   +   +   +   Book/Audios $49.95____

A PARENT'S GUIDE TO TEENAGERS WITH A.D.D.
Video: (90 min) Candice Trudeau, PhD and Dr. Amen explore the problems and solutions of parenting a teenager with ADD. They discuss the impact of ADD teens on the family system and ways to bring about healing. $49.95____
Set Discounts!! Teen Guide Book/Audios, plus Parent's Video $79.95____

ADULT ADD: Video (60 minutes) on the signs, symptoms and treatment for ADD in adults $49.95____

HEALING THE CHAOS WITHIN: The Interaction Between A.D.D., Alcoholism, and Growing Up In An Alcoholic Home
Audio/Workbook Program: Includes a 1 hr audiotape and workbook with checklists questionnaires on ADD, Alcoholism, and Adult Children of Alcoholics. The interaction between these 3 conditions is explained and specific interventions are given for healing the chaos these disorders bring to individuals and families. $29.95____

FIRESTORMS IN THE BRAIN: An Inside Look At Violent Behavior
Video (120 minutes) Learn the latest information on the biology of violent behavior. This video explores genetics, environmental factors, toxic exposures, trauma, substance abuse effects and brain imaging findings in criminally violent individuals. $49.95____

THE INSTRUCTION MANUAL THAT SHOULD HAVE COME WITH YOUR CHILD: New Skills For Frazzled Parents
Book: Includes real stories, handouts, charts, tips, home and school behavior systems, and new section on the "110 Best Things You Can Do For Your Child." $29.95____
Audio Series: (8 tapes) 8 full hours of a complete parent training course taught by Dr. Amen. Step-by-step instructions on superior parenting for difficult and not-so-difficult children and teens. $79.95____
Video: (1 hour 20 min) Dr. Amen LIVE on parenting difficult kids with humor, and practical advice. $49.95____
Set Discounts!!   Book/Audios $89.95____   Book/Video $69.95____
                             The Complete Set of Book/Audios/Video $129.95____

MAKING GOOD DECISIONS:
A Preteen and Teen Guide To Peer Pressure, Sexuality and Drugs
Video (2 hrs): This program is meant to be watched together by parents or group leaders and their pre-teen or teenage children. Includes nine talks (approx 10 min each) between a father and his 12-year-old son about the things parents should tell their kids, but never

do. Topics covered include peer pressure, normal sexual development, teenage pregnancy, AIDS, drugs, and decision making. $39.95____

DON'T SHOOT YOURSELF IN THE FOOT:
A Program To End Self-Defeating Behavior Forever
Book: Includes self-diagnostic quizzes, checklists, exercises, goal sheets, hallmarks of self-defeating and successful behavior, actions and thoughts. Also, instructions on making personalized change self-hypnosis tape. $12.99____
Audio Series: (2 tapes) 2 hours of Dr. Amen LIVE on this topic. $29.95____
Video: (1 hour 20 min) Dr. Amen LIVE on eight prescriptions for success. $49.95____
Set Discounts!!   Book/Audios $37.95____   Book/Video $54.95____
              The Complete Set of Book/Audios/Video $69.95____

MIND COACH:
How To Teach Kids and Teenagers To Think Positively and Feel Good
Book: Everything starts and ends in your mind. MindCoach teaches children and teens how to correct the negative thought patterns which interfere with their lives. It also teaches them how to think in ways that enhance their chances for success in whatever they do. $19.95____
Audio: (2 Tapes, 90 min) Dr. Amen LIVE teaching children how to think positively and feel good. $19.95____
Video: (75 min) Dr. Amen LIVE on teaching children how to think positively and feel good. $49.95____
Set Discounts!!   Book/Audios $29.95____   Book/Video $59.95____

IMAGES INTO THE MIND:
A Radical New Look At Understanding And Changing Behavior
Audio/Book: Brain SPECT Imaging is changing the way we view psychiatric illness. Dr. Amen has been at the forefront of brain imaging research. In this program he shares specific brain patterns which correlate with certain psychiatric conditions (depression, ADD, anxiety, obsessive-compulsive disorder, violence, etc. In addition, based on his research he offers clear prescriptions for healing the mind. Includes a one-hour audiotape and a 189 page book with 30 color SPECT images. $49.95____
Video: (90 minutes) Dr. Amen gives an intimate look into a "working brain." Based on his brain imaging work with over 3,000 patients. $49.95____
Set Discount!!   Book/Audio/Video $89.95____

IMAGES Slide/Text Program (includes 60 color 35mm slides) As Dr. Amen has lectured across the continent to thousands of physicians, mental health professionals, teachers, attorneys, judges and the general public many people have asked him for copies of his slides on brain SPECT imaging. They say it is the images that cause "perceptions to change." In response to those requests he has developed this SPECT program which includes both the slides of actual SPECT images from his clinical practice along with the stories behind the slides. $149.95____

THE SECRETS OF SUCCESSFUL STUDENTS
Book: The skills students need to be successful at school. For 6th graders through graduate school. Includes chapters on organization, getting the most out of teachers, test-taking, homework, writing and speaking skills and much more! $29.95____
Audio Series: (2 tapes) Dr. Amen LIVE on SECRETS $29.95___
Video: (1 hour 18 minutes) Dr. Amen LIVE on SECRETS $49.95____
Set Discounts!!   Book/Audios $49.95____   Book/Video $69.95____

Would You Give TWO MINUTES A DAY For A Lifetime Of Love
Book: This book teaches you how to achieve total focus in your relationship and it gives you the skills to make it happen. $19.95____
Audio: (2 Tapes, 100 min) Dr. Amen LIVE, teaching couples how to achieve total focus in their relationships. $29.95____
Video: (1 hour 20 min) Dr. Amen LIVE on achieving TOTAL FOCUS for relationships. $49.95____
Set Discounts!!   Book/Audios $39.95____   Book/Video $59.95____
                          The Complete Set of Book/Audios/Video $79.95____

TEN STEPS TO BUILDING VALUES WITHIN CHILDREN
Audio/Workbook Program: Includes 2 audiotapes and workbook, giving parents 10 steps to building values within children. Never before are values such an issue in our society. Parents need the best information and this program gives you step-by-step guidelines. $29.95____

THE MOST IMPORTANT THING IN LIFE I LEARNED FROM A PENGUIN!?
A Story On How To Help People Change. Illustrated by Breanne L. Amen
Book: 23 illustrations, plus a second "real life" penguin fable. $12.95____

WHICH BRAIN DO YOU WANT! 24 by 36 inch drug education poster.
This poster compares the brains of a normal person to four drug abusers: a heroin addict, a cocaine abuser, an alcoholic and a chronic marijuana abuser. Through the use of brain SPECT studies, sophisticated blood flow and activity maps of the brain, the poster shows startling differences between the normal brain and those of the substance abusers. The poster was developed to educate people on the real effects of drugs on the brain.
The full size 24 by 36 inch poster is $15____

Library Discounts

Buy A Library of Dr. Amen's Materials And Save Over $500.00!! The total for all products (except Clinician's Guide To ADD and Images Slide Set), using set discounts, is over $1100. We would like to offer you the complete library for only: $600 (S&H included free). With a purchase of $200 or more, the Clinicians Guide To ADD Series may be purchased for $50 off at $149.95 for video series and $79.95 for audio series.

Ways To Order

Telephone orders: Toll Free: (800) 626-2720 ext 400.   Have your Visa, Amex, MasterCard ready   (24hrs)

Fax orders: (707) 429-8210 (24 hours a day)

Postal orders: MindWorks Press, 350 Chadbourne Road, Fairfield, CA 94585
(707) 429-7181

Product	Price	Quantity	Total
Subtotal			
Tax (7.25% in California)			
Shipping & Handling (for domestic orders add 10%, for international orders add 20%)			
Total			

Name:	
Address:	
Phone #:	
Credit Card Type:	**Credit Card #**
Signature (for CC orders only):	

Call or write for a full color catalog.
Purchase Orders are accepted.
Volume Discounts available. Please Call.

Please write us with your comments and suggestions. We look forward to hearing from you.